Connecting

Wall Street and

The Federal Reserve

The connection between the Big Banks of Wall Street
and their creation.

The Federal Reserve

Written

By

G. I. Pinto

"Let me issue and control a nation's money and I care not who writes the laws." Mayer Amschel Rothschild (1744-1812), founder of the House of Rothschild.

Index

Introduction

In our present world, people, with higher education, live, thinking what is happening around the world. Those people without higher education sometimes wonder what happens. Both groups though remain unaware of whom shapes events around the world. We will discuss the controversial presidency of Woodrow Wilson. President Wilson is the starting point in helping shape the most important events in the twentieth century and beyond. We find in his administration more lies and deceit of greater effect than your average Presidential administration. This is essential to understand the world we live today. He cultivated close relations with wicked characters such as Bernard Baruch, Colonel Mandel House. He developed intimate relations with the Network of Zionist bankers. Wilson became a collaborator of the Zionist agenda, and he brought an unfair advantage to the global elite. If you lack this knowledge, the actions of those who dominate the U.S. government and the Western world do not make sense. Gain this knowledge for everything falls into place.

I must warn you. This journey is going to shake your foundation and your beliefs. You cannot close your mind, but must show some backbone. If you believe what you read, and watch on TV as political reality; this book is not for you. Once you discover how the deceivers perform their magic, the comfort of ignorance is no longer possible. Once you let the truth change your view, you're not coming back to your old ways.

Carroll Quigley, the respected historian was privy to documents banned to us. In his book "Tragedy and Hope" he explained the ruling of the most powerful and deceitful political scheme. Somehow, Quigley learned to admire these skillful and manipulative immoral men. They are responsible for taking control of our freedom and democracy. Quigley's book is extensive, but it will show us "these small groups controlling the world want to dominate all habitable portions of the world." We will learn the Zionist elite controls it all. Let us make it clear that disclosing the Zionist does not mean anti-Semitic. First, they are not of Semitic blood. These Zionists throughout history have used methods of deception, theft, and violence. They have achieved more toward world domination than any rulers in human history have.

Like other authors of Woodrow Wilson, I do not wish to be flamboyant. I want this book to be simple to read. Still, packed with some of the most MIND-BLOWING historical information you have ever read. Everything I bring is of public domain. Yet, if we do not connect the dots is where we miss their true purpose. This information stands so close to us that we cannot see. We need to step out of the forest to look what's around you. Throughout this book, I make many citations that you can say....I heard it from the Horse's Mouth! A reader like you who strives to know the truth, and nothing but the truth, will enjoy this book. I remember, as a student, in history class, felt like I was getting the sanitized version only. It's my experience to see many would rather remain oblivious to the truth than confronting it. If you are seeking the truth you want to break the mold of many. I have broken the fence and my mind is free. This book can help you set your path to freedom too. I share something that I learned some time ago from the German author and philosopher Riedrich Nietzche:

"The surest way to corrupt a youth is to teach him or her to hold in higher esteem those who think alike than those who think differently."

This book is not another scholarly biography on the life of the 28th President of the United States, Woodrow Wilson. It's the blue collar explanation to a white-collar crime. Wilson's administration had a series of uncommon events that speeded up the Zionist agenda. These events have brought thus, serious and enormous effects that we can feel today. Many scholars have written about Wilson's accomplishments. They have called the Federal Reserve his greatest achievement. Nevertheless, these scholars have failed to write the truth of creating the Federal Reserve. On December 23, 1913 America suffered a coup d'état when in the name of the fraud, Congress passed into law creating the Federal Reserve. The few voices in Congress that opposed this takeover knew what it meant for the nation, but the Zionist duped or forced them into silence.

December 23, 1913 is the day that should live in infamy. The New York bankers, the Money Trust perpetrated the biggest crime of the twentieth century. President Woodrow Wilson took part in it by signing it into law. On that day, we should be remembering President Wilson to the Zionist bankers instead. The coup d'état consisted in taking control of the United States currency, or the money supply. With that awesome limitless power in private hands, they can manipulate everybody and everything.

It's time for us to reveal events the Zionists have kept in the dark for too long. It's time to bring it to light. Trying to expose it creates a problem for the Zionists. We know they are the big monster out there. Big brother controlling everything, and every part of our lives. However, this monster, this T-Rex, has blood, and it's cold blood is money. Once we take the money away T-Rex will die of money starvation. First, our enemy is in the shadows need to know who he/she is. We need to know who we are fighting against. We need to learn the truths denied to us. But this time we will not forget; we will sear it in our minds Woodrow Wilson greatest achievement is in truth his greatest curse. One hundred years have passed and either we ignore or forget this piece of important American history. Usually is the lack of accurate education that, the Zionist would want to keep from you. The public in general hardly remembers Woodrow Wilson, including our youth. The public in general have no idea who created the Federal Reserve and why. Do you think they know it has the power to create money out of thin air? How the Federal

Reserve loans this funny money to the government at interest? By taking control of the money supply the Federal Reserve is the master and we are the slaves. Its influence has tide a noose around your neck to believe it is only natural because you have had it all your life.

It's a terrifying fact. All Americans should be aware of this important part of American history. The authors, the experts we count on choose to omit it to keep us in the dark. No schoolbooks has any of this information available. A small minority of teachers know it, a few would teach it. Scholars continue to write great biographies about President Woodrow Wilson. Yet, not one dares confront the greatest curse he has left for us. It seems like if they are paying them for not touching this important theme. Any scholar dedicated to study the life of Woodrow Wilson would know the role he played in creating the Federal Reserve. Plus, what a dismal failure the Federal Reserve has been in keeping our economy stable. Our society complies within a predetermined circle of ideas. We happily to ignore what is true because it does not fit our pattern of ideas. The Wilson scholars prefer not to say anything. They opt not to write what can hurt their careers. Lucky for us, we are not afraid to rock the boat a little bit. Nothing is going to stop us from learning what we need to know if we want to recognize and fight this monster. The following pages contain information that most of the public in general has never seen before. It is like pulling the band out of your eyes, or getting your head removed from the sand. I know... it can be painful... But have the courage to continue reading; this book might open your eyes just enough. You need to continue searching, learning, and finding out the truth. We need to become more concern citizens. We need to learn how to ask the right questions. We need to start demanding from our politicians to repeal the Federal Reserve. It's the most important issue of our time. If controlling the money supply means everything to them. It's just as important to take it back. But we don't have that resolve just yet. Why not? It's because we know too little on the subject, and they know too much. In the words of the economics Nobel Prize winner Milton Friedman: Money is too much of a serious matter to leave it to the central bankers.

Chapter 1

Who was President Woodrow Wilson?

Thomas Woodrow Wilson was the 28th President of the United States from 1913 to 1921 and leader of the Progressive Movement. He served as President of Princeton University from 1902 to 1910. Woodrow Wilson with a PhD in political science was a college professor who turned politician by some strange fate. As a politician, Wilson started his career, joining the progressive movement of America. This movement began in the middle of the nineteenth century and continue into the first half of the twentieth century. The Progressive movement was the answer to the deep changes of industrial modernization. Besides, America was seeing the growth of steel production and railroads into large corporations. Nevertheless, the nations' most important issue was the fear of corruption in American politics. Therefore, the Progressive movement was necessary to address all the deep changes facing in America. So, for Woodrow Wilson at the center of his political believes was to be mindful for corruption in American politics. For this, Wilson wanted to expose and end the corruption. In 1911 during his presidential campaign, Wilson delivered speeches that would certify his beliefs and what would want to change or avoid for America. Here is an extract of his speeches coming from the new Freedom: A Call for the Emancipation of the Generous Energies of a People," published in 1913. "The New Freedom" is a distillation of campaign speeches Wilson made while running for President in 1911. On page 185, there is the following section:

"A great industrial nation is controlled by its system of credit. Our system of credit is privately concentrated. The growth of the nation, therefore, and all our activities are in the hands of a few men who, even if their action be honest and intended for the public interest,

are necessarily concentrated upon the great undertakings in which their own money is involved and who necessarily, by very reason of their own limitations, chill and check and destroy genuine economic freedom."

In this speech Wilson is clear and aware the nation's industries are already under the clutches of credit. He adds, private hands control it. In other words, Wilson is talking about the New York banks, also known as the Money Trust. Woodrow Wilson as for other politicians made their political platform to talk about braking the grip of the Money Trust. History tells us the politicians run campaigns proposing to brake the grip of the Money Trust. What we don't know is that they use this elaborated ruse just to win the elections. What we find even more ALARMING! Even MINDBOGGLING! Is that Woodrow Wilson says that they can chill, check, and destroy genuine economic freedom.

Wow! Woodrow… This is deep stuff.

It's clear Woodrow Wilson understood the risks our nation was running into, and he was not about to let it continue. Following the Progressive rules he would either put a stop to it or at least try to change direction. At least, we can interpret this as a warning issued by the candidate Wilson. The same Wilson who later as President would turn on his party's beliefs first, and then his people to do exactly the opposite. This speech is Wilson's famous quote that has traveled throughout world. Nonetheless, the quote is not true sorry to say. The idea was to make the public and the whole world believe that Woodrow Wilson regretted signing of the FED into law. Someone took it to task to compose his speeches into one quote to give us this impression. The second part of the quote belongs to another speech he made. After that we will see Wilson's quote is the product of two speeches put together.

The New Freedom: A Call for the Emancipation of the Generous Energies of a People," published in 1913. On page 201:

"We are at the parting of the ways. We have not one or two or three, but many, established and formidable monopolies in the United States. We have, not one or two, but many, fields of endeavor into which it is difficult, if not impossible, for the independent man to enter. We have restricted credit, we have restricted opportunity, we have controlled development, and we have come to be one of the worst ruled, one of the most completely controlled and dominated, governments in the civilized world — no longer a government by the opinion and the duress of small groups of dominant men."

We can identify some members of the small group of dominant men. We can start with the Rothschild in banking, the Rockefeller, and the Mellon in oil, the Astor in real estate. We can also add the Carnegie and Schwab in steel, the Harriman, Stanford, and Vanderbilt in railroad just to mention a few. Zionism is an ideology that runs deep and strong among these families. We must keep in mind, as they were powerful then, they remain in power now. The most influential and self-appointed banker of the time was JP Morgan. Because of the weight of these families' fortunes and influence, they all began to seek out JP Morgan. He was the banker of choice.

For a moment, just to satisfy your curiosity you like to be a fly on the ceiling. To hear the banking cartel commenting in secret about Woodrow Wilson's speech. They might have said. You haven't seen nothing yet... Surely, you can see Wilson had a good grasp of the political and economic conditions America was facing. He knew if continue this course, it would be the end of America as a free nation. When, Wilson gave this speech though. Senator Nelson Aldrich and his banker cronies from New York had already gone to Jekyll Island. There, after nine days of fake duck hunting they came back with a piece of proposed legislation for creating a Central Bank the Federal Reserve. It's important to point out that before the Federal Reserve was in effect Woodrow Wilson is denouncing the existence of monopolies in our nation. This anomaly by definition is unacceptable in a free economy. Still, there they were big monopolies; alive and strong and Woodrow Wilson is saying it.

Out-laud! These are his words!

"Because these monopolies, it's next to impossible for the independent man to compete, and rightfully so, this would cause lack of credit and opportunity to those entrepreneurs seeking out better opportunities and credit."

In the words of the Standard Oil tycoon John D. Rockefeller said. "Competition is a Sin." Of course it is... Rockefeller. It made sense for him to unite with the rest of the banking cartel to create the biggest monopoly on Earth. For Rockefeller and his cronies this was the greatest unfair opportunity of the century. This was a dream come true for the Zionists banker's. Rockefeller is among the founders of the shameful Federal Reserve. Woodrow Wilson has made the right assessment up to this point in history. He is telling us according to his information this is the shape of our industrial foundation. You just cannot dream up or make up these conditions. The monopolies were already well settled, and he knows the horrendous effects that they bring up to the common person. In Wilson's view, mine, and perhaps a few more people that voted for him. "We have come to be one of the worst ruled, one of the most completely controlled and dominated, governments in the civilized world."

These are tall and dire words he spelled for us.

Nevertheless, why the US Congress or the newspapers didn't take a stand we can ask. There were many people who heard him saying these speeches. I guess it never registered. There were people like Congressman Charles A. Lindbergh on the eve of passing the law.

"This Act establishes the most gigantic trust on earth....When the President signs this Act, the invisible government by the Money

Power, proven to exist by the Money Trust Investigation, will be legalized....The money power overawes the legislative and executive forces of the Nation and of the States. I have seen these forces exerted during the different stages of this bill...." (Congressman Charles A. Lindbergh, referring to the act which established the Federal Reserve. Congressional Record, Vol. 51, p. 1446. December 22, 1913.

Lindbergh knew how horrendous would be passing the Federal Reserve into law. Yet, except for a few lonely voices on December 23, 1913, late at night. While Congress was nearly asleep, they passed it. President Wilson cheerfully signed it. Well, by this single act Woodrow Wilson surrendered the most awesome power the US government had the control of the money supply.

In Wilson's mind, this was already a done deal, for he considered our form of government obsolete. The United States of America is no longer the land of the Free and the Home of the Brave. What is more shocking is that Wilson refers about the Money Trust. The same people who helped him become president. Woodrow Wilson knew back then that we are under the duress of a small group of dominant men. In other words, the Money Trust of New York controlling the economy, Congress the White House and beyond.

Is there any reason at all to believe otherwise?

NO!.. One emphatically and unquestionably NO!

Because of Wilson's actions these are the conditions which we live today. Wilson was not trying to be prophetic in his speeches. He was aware of how ruthless and harmful the bankers can be for the economy. The Money Trust bankrolled the biggest monopolies. Meanwhile, behind the scenes, as the Zionists like to work. The

Banking Cartel was moving in, with stealth and focused, unstoppable in their purpose. With unlimited wealth and collaborators at their command they knew it's only a matter of time. They wanted to achieve again that crown jewel, The Central Bank refuted by President Andrew Jackson.

In 1836 Old Hickory repealed the Second National Bank of the United States. Immediately after. Just to show you how insidious these people are. Nicholas Biddle the head manager of the Second US Bank threatened with a depression and said:

"This worthy President thinks that because he has scalped Indians and imprisoned judges, he is to have his way with the bank. He is mistaken."

More on that Later! Now, let's see what someone did with President Woodrow Wilson's speeches. This is the famous Wilson's quote the whole world knows.

"I am a most unhappy man. I have unwittingly ruined my country. A great industrial nation is controlled by its system of credit. Our system of credit is concentrated. The growth of the nation, therefore, and all our activities are in the hands of a few men. We have come to be one of the worst ruled, one of the most completely controlled and dominated Governments in the civilized world no longer a Government by free opinion, no longer a Government by conviction and the vote of the majority, but a Government by the opinion and duress of a small group of dominant men"

As you can see, this is a clear composition of two speeches. The added "I am a most unhappy man" it's just made up. It sounds good and believable. It sounds presidential since its a direct copy from his campaign speeches. Sounds scholarly, as something Wilson could have said. Still, is not true, surely you can see that. The purpose is to seek the truth and expose deception. I don't understand why go through so much time and trouble to give the impression that he regretted signing the Federal Reserve into law. To think about it, sounds more like if somebody intents to clear him. If you look this quote carefully, it goes with those scholars who write beautifully about Wilson. You know the type, those who neglect to write about the most devastating scourge he left us with. And to make matters worse, Wilson was proud of his shameful deed. But to further the fraud someone has to make him look good in the pages of history. After all the bankers owe him all the power they enjoy today. Although they might say. Oh! But we helped in getting him elected. Yes, but you turned him into your poppet, and you have received payback beyond the dreams of greed.

I don't know who put this quote together and perhaps there is no way to find out. I suspect is the same people who writes scholarly biographies about him. I would argue. Rather than make us believe that he repented from the most insidious legislation in the history of the United States. I wish they could have just come up with something more relevant, like the truth for example. I know the truth is a rare commodity now days, but I have news for you. The truth can be and has been manipulated by the elite. Therefore, we must not expect any truth from them. We must seek it out ourselves. So, it shouldn't surprise us. It is important to know the mind and character of Woodrow Wilson. That's why we need to know his religious and ethical disposition. We know that his father was a minister in the First Presbyterian Church. As a result, that made him a person of strong faith, and personal convictions. We know he didn't change his mind so easily, and he limited his love only for the people of his own race. Wilson earned the title of a racist even by the standards of his time. This is what you call KKK material.

What a charming fellow!

In his youth, young Woodrow Wilson must have spent many days at the dinner table with his father and mother in Staunton, Virginia. His father, as a true preacher must have quoted him the bible often. This was young Woodrow's moral compass and guidance to the world he lived-in. Thanks to his religious upbringing young Woodrow understood is because God's will the world is like it is. God has explained this to us in the bible you see. Take Leviticus 25:44 it says: your male and female slaves are to come from the nations around you; from them you may buy slaves. And so on and on. It's a terrible picture for a young mind to believe it's true. Pick up your bible, you can look it up yourself. If the bible says that you can buy slaves from other nations around you. It's possible they could be from another race. In the shameful case of the United States the black race. Tragically, the bible made it acceptable. Wilson could not go against the word of God. For Wilson this is all the justification you need to feel good and no conflict with slavery, racism and the word of God. It's not too farfetched. This is indoctrination young Woodrow Wilson received in his early days. Let's not lose sight of the scenarios where the events of the Bible happened were in northeast Africa if I am not mistaken. This is where the indigenous people were black like the ancient Egyptians. Woodrow Wilson a stubborn racist made him a poor excuse for a Virginian. Much too far to fit the shoes of Patrick Henry.

About his renowned Nobel Peace prize in 1920. Wilson's recognition as a Peacemaker is debatable. Let us look at the Nobel price, where it comes from, and how it began. Alfred Nobel was a Swedish chemist and a skillful entrepreneur and businessperson. Born in Stockholm on October 21, 1833 he invents dynamite in 1866. His father was Immanuel Nobel an engineer and inventor. He set up an engineering and weapons company in St. Petersburg, Russia. Like father and son, they both liked to see things blown up. But more important I think they recognized how profitable the weapons business was. We remember Alfred Nobel for using his personal fortune to create the Nobel Foundation. From here, he would award

Nobel Prizes to those who benefit humanity. Do you think that he benefited humanity? This is ironic for Alfred Nobel to say the least. Some people say that he created this foundation to ease his conscious. That may be true. Seemingly he was a man of peace, but for a man of peace he had a strange way to make a living. Doesn't it strike you strange the man who creates a dynamite also creates the most prestigious Peace prize? How do you make this to pass scrutiny? Somebody should have said: Alfred, do you think that this is a good idea?

A Peace Prize in your name; after all, thanks to your invention we can kill people more effectively you know. As a result, President Woodrow Wilson gets the Nobel Piece Prize in 1920. Meanwhile Europe was knee-deep in blood after World War I. What chills my bones is how he's picked for such an honor when the guy took us to war! Reluctant or not, but led us into war, and the US Army must have killed tenths of thousands of human beings in a war of Zionist design. An honest and fair Foundation should have banned him period. Woodrow Wilson Wilson Piece Prize is like giving Julius Caesar the Peace Price after he massacred Gaul. He came back to Rome triumphant after killing better than eight hundred thousand people who didn't want war or anything to do with Rome. What about this piece making example. When Pharaoh sent Moses to Ethiopia because he feared there would be war. Moses came back triumphant not because he waged war killed his enemies and conquered Ethiopia. Moses was triumphant because he signed an alliance with their king. Now, that's more like it. Don't you think? We cannot say the same of Woodrow Wilson. Can we? Back in 1915 the Zionist Bernard Baruch knew already the United States would take part in WWI. He and his Zionist cronies must have decided about Wilson. He will get the United States into war. He will win it for us, will sign the League of Nations which is our main goal, and we'll give him the Nobel Peace Prize. That's how it happened. WWI spelled great success for the Zionist agenda, However, they missed on the League of Nations. Immediately after though, the Zionist began plans to have WWII. The goal was to finally bring about the Zionist UN as a prelude for one world government the New World Order. This is what President George Busch said on September 11, 1991. Back to Wilson, he gets us into war, gets the Nobel Peace Prize, and the people cheered. For the Nobel Peace Prize is nothing but blood money. Woodrow Wilson if he had a shred of decency might have reflected and wouldn't have accepted this prize. If I were Wilson, holding that medal and that big check in my hand. I think I would've said. I have earned this prize with the blood of my dearest fellow compatriots. I hold in my hands the blood of my enemies that yesterday I called my friends. It just doesn't fit the deed. It just wouldn't feel right. To think that Woodrow Wilson promised the American people to keep them out of the war and secure their freedom. No President, a gentleman, and a scholar should have received a Peace Prize bought with the blood and guts of your fellowman... Does that sound right to you?

These are the results that you get when you exchange precious blood for cheap ink. Because we do not practice of connecting the dots. Because we are either too gullible or indifferent today we see President Obama getting the Nobel Piece Prize. "For his extraordinary efforts to strengthen international diplomacy and cooperation between peoples".

Are you kidding me?

Meanwhile, Our troops acting as cannon fodder for the Zionist are exercising aggressive diplomacy in Afghanistan. Way to go Obama. Some Peace Prize you got.

For a moment, let's be gentle and softhearted and think the Nobel Prize is a noble recognition. A means to recognize the excellence of men and women who work hard for the benefit of humanity. But not peace, please, that's making a bad condition worse. Usually, details in history like this escape the average person who is more dormant than aware. The average person is more concern about making a paycheck, watching the game or playing video games. People in general knows little about the history that changed the world. That's why you are here working your neurons a little extra this time for your benefit though. Together we connect the dots so we can keep the spineless politicians from acting in the name of the Zionist fraud, lies, and deceit. We The People cannot continue in the same path of deception the sleeper must awaken beginning with you.

The respected historian John Milton Cooper wrote a wonderful biography about Woodrow Wilson. It's my belief this how he benefits his career and gets rewards from the Zionist press. This is the review Cooper received from the Boston Globe:

"Cooper's much-anticipated biography finally gives Wilson his due. The preeminent living historian of Wilson and his era, Cooper has studied the man and his times for decades...he now presents us with his magnum opus. The book is deeply, indeed exhaustively researched, and beautifully, often movingly narrated. It is far and away the best biography of the 28th president we have, and as such it is unlikely to be surpassed."

Boston Globe

Here is another review, equally spectacular!

"Cooper's monumental new biography seeks to revive Wilson for the 21st century—not simply to narrate a presidential life, but to explain why he deserves our national esteem....An admiring and engaging work of presidential revisionism.... A powerful, deeply researched and highly readable case for keeping Wilson in the top ranks of American presidents."

New York Times Book Review

Are you serious!

This can only happen if newspapers like the Boston Globe and the New York Times are under Zionist control. Is that possible? Let's see. First, the Boston Globe and the New York Times are both the property of Mr. Arthur Ochs Sulzberger, CEO. He and his grandfather, Arthur Hays Sulzberger had been members of the (CFR) Council on Foreign Relations. The CFR is the closest contraption to a Zionist headquarter in Washington D.C. and New York. Therefore, with a controlled press like this you stand no chance at getting a fair review if what you're trying to do is expose the truth. We should realize that freedom of speech is just possible if you own the press. It's self-evident that he who controls the printing press controls the thinking of the age. On the hand, for a historian like John Cooper, who has studied Woodrow Wilson for decades. Is inconceivable to miss the single most important event of his political career. Creating the Federal Reserve and its horrendous results such as signing the American people into Zionist slavery. What is keeping Cooper from addressing these important issues? Other authors like Cooper who have written at length about Woodrow Wilson have all missed the mark by a mile. Why can't they have an independent voice for a change? Do they think that WE THE PEOPLE do not have the stomach for it? Or maybe they are afraid exposing the true nature of the Federal Reserve might cause the people to rise and protest the tyranny in which we live? They must think skeletons of us, not because we are dead, but because they think we don't have the guts.

Patrick Henry the great Virginian, once said: "Give me liberty or give me death".

Americans would rather die than live in chuckles but only if they realize it. The Zionist genius have managed to chuckled our minds through politics and religion. The only way they can continue with this deception is by using people like Cooper and his critics. They can back a great piece of biographical work about Wilson. Yet, neglect the information critical for understanding current events.

Why can Cooper muster the guts to write like John Galbraith. He wrote an acerbic analysis of the nation's concentration of private wealth in just a few hands. In the decade of the 1950s Galbraith went against the establishment and wrote prophetically about the dangers of deregulating the financial markets. I know someone who wasn't listening; Alan Greenspan, the FED chairman and a Zionist. He was Mr. Deregulation himself. Thanks to his stupid market deregulation. His belief the market will correct itself; created the biggest economic bubble that burst in 2008. John Galbraith wrote about corporate greed and the inattention to the cost of our military power. I know who was listening; President Eisenhower (CFR). In his farewell speech he warned us against one of the unfavorable results of WWII. The mighty military complex. He said "if not kept in check, it could also become the means of our destruction." Well, since only a hand full could pick up his meaning, his speech passed to history unattended until now. As a result, we have a Zionist infiltrated military complex. So powerful and so pervasive that nobody dares to challenge. Today there are powerful Zionist contractors that feed of the Pentagon rich budget. They are so entrenched that now is difficult to tell them apart.

I am sorry if you think I am picking on Cooper. Others have written about Wilson too, I know. But if you engage in the task to write such a monumental opus. To bring the Wilson's figure to the twenty-first century you should do it to enlighten people rather than give them more of the same. Don't engage in pages of superfluous events that will not help to know Wilson and what he stood for. I know, Copper like the other authors have fallen prey of the establishment. It's a proven fact, these authors can be men well trained, and skilled with a PhD from a prominent university. Still, the majority remain in the dark, where just a few have seen the light. They find themselves more receptive to the Zionist order. More conditioned and interested in keeping their reputations and advance their careers. The problem is the present global order. It works on a foundation of omission, deception and lies. The present scheme has done nothing but destabilized the values of individuals and families. Damaging the core of a healthy society weakens its fabrics making it more susceptible to demands principally from government.

Thomas Jefferson our American Renaissance man. Once described the press as the fourth *branch in government. He wrote:*

"The basis of our government being the opinion of the people, the very first object should be to keep that right; and were it left to me to decide whether we should have a government without newspapers, or newspapers without a government, I should not hesitate a moment to prefer the latter."

Is Thomas Jefferson Something or what!

Why don't we heed these words of wisdom Why our leaders and politicians ignore it Or choose to dismiss it? It's pure whole journalism that should be the holy grail to protect our democracy and republic. The reason they dismiss it is because politicians have sold out to the Zionist, they are just banker's pawns. Thomas Jefferson was talking about was honest newspapers run by honest and truthful journalist. The problem with universities today is that they no longer teach you how to think what to think. The schools of journalists express more interest in coloring your thinking than freeing your mind. They don't want to teach you how to be that fourth power in government. As a journalist you first and main duty should be to report events truthfully and independently. Only then a journalist can feel part of the fourth power in government Jefferson talked about. Today the journalists are just storytellers of the controlled mass-media. They are a product of the teachings of Edward Bernays, the Zionist propaganda King. Bernays started in trying to manipulate public opinion using the psychology of the subconscious. He thought manipulation was necessary in society, which he regarded. "As irrational and dangerous as a result of the herd instinct." You see what I mean! To the Zionist we are nothing but a herd of mindless or at best limited capacities creatures.

Today Bernays' techniques are the method of choice in the Art and Science of Public Relations. The Zionist applies this knowledge to manipulate our society through the news media, and the Internet. As a result, the news media as a whole have done a masterful job in keeping us in the dark while they have neglected to tell the public and educate. David Rockefeller said it at the Bilderburg meeting in Baden-Baden, Germany in 1991.

"We are grateful to the Washington Post, The New York Times, Time Magazine and other great publications whose directors have attended our meetings and respected their promises of discretion for almost forty years."
It would have been impossible for us to develop our plan for the world if we had been subjected to the lights of publicity during those years. But, the world is now more sophisticated and prepared to march towards a world government. The supranational sovereignty of an intellectual elite and world bankers is surely preferable to the national auto-determination practiced in past centuries." David Rockefeller, Bilderberg meeting 1991

Do you need any more proof?

The media Tycoons have become peddlers of deception and fraud. They stand guilty of reducing the minds of the public to "a state of impotent confusion". It was John D. Rockefeller, who wanted a nation of workers not thinkers.   Knowing that this would help advance his goals. He helped to create the foundation to organize the education system in the United "States.

You think he got his way?

In retrospective, It makes sense. You see... As Wood Wilson so eloquently described it. Our nation is under the duress of a small group of dominant men. Therefore, Rockefeller and his cronies had to take control of the press and education in the United States. Otherwise, they would've risked exposure by those genuine journalists committed to the truth. Shame nobody had the courage or wisdom to blow the whistle on these gangsters. Anybody could have stopped them from achieving their deceitful plans. The time has come to pay attention and watch like a hawk every elected politician. Are you getting this? We need to remind our Senators and Representative that they work for the American taxpayer not the Zionist lobbyist in Washington. We need to remind them we want our money's worth and if they cannot stand the heat, then, get out of the kitchen. We need to tell them "Either lead, follow or get out the way". We have put too much trust on people that just don't deserve it.

Chapter 2

How Did He Climb to Power?

Because you should know that history repeats itself. Electing Woodrow Wilson for president of the United States had no chance to succeed in the eyes of the American people. Just like Barrack Obama had no chance against the party anointed candidate Hillary Clinton. Just like Woodrow Wilson and Bernard Baruch. Barack Obama long before entering politics, he received his political indoctrination from another notorious Zionist. Dr. Zbigniew Brzezinski of Columbia University. His book "Between Two Ages" served to inspire David Rockefeller to build the Trilateral Commission in 1973. Brzezinski is also a CFR member (Council on Foreign Relations) and a prominent figure for the New World Order. Do I need to say any more? After Barack Obama received proper indoctrination he became the puppet of the Zionist Zbig Brzezinski and the banks of New York. It's no secret the banks poured large amounts of money to elect our beloved President Obama to the White House. They now expect a return on their investment. Obama indebted and compromised, has the duty to safeguard, and to keep the Federal Reserve intact, untouched and above the law. The Zionists are constantly projecting their power and influence. If we could only pay attention to details. We could learn how they work. For instance, we have young Americans training to fight back cyber-attacks for our intelligence agencies. What they don't know is that those intelligence agencies are under Zionist control. That's where the deception lays.

Let's go back to 2008. When the economic crisis burst Tim Geithner was the chairperson of the Federal Reserve in New York, the most important branch of Federal Reserve as a whole. Do you think he had anything to do with the crisis? Do you think he was submissive while surrounded by all those Giga Banks of New York? We need to understand the Giga Banks of New York work in unison with the Federal Reserve because they own the Federal Reserve. In essence they are the Federal Reserve. Yet Obama calls Geithner to be his Secretary of the Treasury. Based on whose recommendations? Larry Summers and Robert Rubin. Both are hard core Zionist with a well-earned reputation for being crooks. Larry Summers, Robert Rubin and Tim Geithner are all birds of the feather. Therefore, to call Tim Geithner to fix the economy is like seeing the farmer asking the hawk to protect the henhouse.

Are you serious?

Why do we miss this point? Why the press corp and the authorities fail to notice? It's because we live in apathy, we are not in the habit of connecting the dots. We allowed it to happen because we don't know who the enemy is. We think a Federal Reserve chairperson should do a great job as a Secretary of the Treasury; after all they all are part of the Federal Government. Right? Wrong!! Would you have let Al Capone be the administrator of the City of Chicago? Of course not, but that's what we did through Congress when we let Tim take over the Treasury. You might think: you cannot say that of Tim Geithner! He never broke the law, he's an honorable man. Well, he chaired for a crooked, and unscrupulous organization. What does that make you?

So, when Obama moved to the White house in the middle of the economic debacle he gets the Zionist's choice Timothy Geithner. Tim the banker worked for Goldman Sachs, one of the worse reputable banks. At Goldman Sachs, Tim trained to become chairperson of the Federal Reserve in New York. In the middle of the economic crisis Tim gets a promotion from Robert Rubin. He is to become Treasury Secretary for Barrack Obama. Rubin a Zionist and ex-secretary of the Treasury under Bill Clinton. The Zionist follows procedure. They bring their own people to cover key positions. As they did with Woodrow Wilson so they did with Obama. After Wilson signed the Federal Reserve into law, they brought Benjamin Strong to become the first Federal Reserve chairperson. Strong was an acquaintance and a friend of Woodrow Wilson. And for Obama they brought their boy Timothy Geithner for Secretary of the Treasury. In other words, Obama is just the king poppet, but the Zionist pulls the strings. It made no difference in the aisles of Congress if Tim cheated or was late paying his taxes; he still made it and got the confirmation.

Can it get any crazier than that!

To reemphasize you have Tim Geithner, chairman of the Federal Reserve in New York. He gets a promotion from Robert Rubin for Secretary of the Treasury. During his Congressional confirmation it turns out that Tim happens to be a deadbeat because he can't even pay his taxes on time. Still, he gets the nomination? The Zionists must feel omnipotent to think that they can pull a stunt like that. This can only happen if the Zionist know that we live in apathy that we just couldn't care less one way or the other. And they are right. For an old Roman proverb said: "If you're getting screwed is because you deserved it." For you and I the average citizen if our credit reports don't score high enough, you don't get the mortgage, the car or the job. Now days; if your Facebook page is not agreeable to your potential employer; you don't get the job. Never mind if you don't pay your taxes, but pretty boy Tim landed the job of his life. What's going on here? You see... This is what Woodrow Wilson meant during his campaign speeches when he said. "We are governed by a small group of dominant men."

Tim Geithner, the Goldmanite, and an Federal Reserve affiliate. Has dedicated his heart, mind and soul for the benefit of the Banking Cartel. Do you think is going to bring that same dedication for the people of the United States at the snap of your fingers? Are the members of Congress delusional to believe in Geithner's loyalty? Are we the people of the United States delusional to believe Geithner would help us? If we pay attention to details this is another example that Congress is under the duress of a few dominant men; the Zionist lobby. But, this little Zionist shenanigan unlike other tricks get out in the open you'll see. On July 3, 2009 a reporter asked Paul Craig Roberts, the former US Assistant Secretary of the Treasury. "Does the US Secretary of the Treasury work for the people or does he work for the banking system on Wall Street? To which he replied. "Geithner works for Goldman Sachs."

They smacked us for gullible, but the Zionist are not sorry, they expect you to like it. They feel they can pee on us without even bothering to call it rain. We can explain with the following. There is a Banking Cartel in-charge of controlling the money supply of The United States. This is the Federal Reserve working in collaboration with the Giga Banks of New York. They kindly sends us pretty boy Timmy to help us solve the problems that they created to begin with.

Wow! If this is not shameless I don't know what is.

Perhaps you need to know this. Tim Geithner worked with fellow Goldmanite Henry Paulson the outgoing Secretary of the Treasury. Together they bailed out their beloved Goldman Sachs bank and all the culprit banks. I suppose when you work at this level the question of loyalty becomes irrelevant. When it comes to serving your country, whether as a soldier or Secretary of the Treasury your choice is clear. It's not clear for the globalist Zionist bankers because they don't feel love for our country they can only feel greed. The point being is that this couldn't unless Obama was under orders to bring Tim Geithner on board. The Banking Cartel proves once again the coup d'état of 1913 is alive and well. The Oval Office is belongs to them to control not for Obama or any future president. So, it shouldn't be a surprise for us to see President Obama proposing to increase the powers of the Federal Reserve. According to him. Obama would make this proposal to avoid an economic disaster once again. But his proposal had no punch. It voted to add some Mickey mouse rules on the smaller banks, but left the big banks intact. Their game will continue. If Obama wanted to make good on his promise to change America, he would have proposed to reinstate the Glass-Steagall Act. That law has punching power, and can make a difference. Nonetheless, This is the spectacle that makes your jaw drop about three inches. When you hear this nonsense, this absurdity coming from the president of the United States. This can only happen when you're blinded and you just don't understand what Federal Reserve scam is. You think; well, that sound like a good idea. The sad fact is the Federal Reserve does not need permission or authority from Obama or Congress to increase its powers., The Federal Reserve swayed Congress and tricked them to place it above the law. Any attempt at meaningful auditing is just not possible. That's what makes it extremely dangerous, and utterly wrong. In an interview by PBS Allan Greenspan received this question. "what should be the proper relationship between the chairman of the Federal Reserve and the President of the United States". He answered.

"Well firstable the Federal Reserve is an independent agency, and that means basically that there is no agency in government which can overrule actions that we take. So long that this is in place and there is no evidence that the administration or the Congress or anybody else is requesting that we do things other than what we think is the appropriate thing, then what the relationships are don't frankly matter."

This not only devastating news, but Greenspan cannot get any clearer than this.

Do you see how absurd Obama's statement is? President Obama deserves a good briefing about this fact. Don't you think he should know what the Federal Reserve is all about? Not if you're surrounded by Zionist. His staff, mostly Zionist Instead, rather than helping the president, the leader of the so called Free World, allow him to make a fool out of himself. Of course, this was just rhetoric, a demagogue speech, aimed to the ignorant populace is that simple.

For Obama or any president in the future who wants to make changes in America must take care of first things first. It means nothing short of taking back control of the money supply and put it the hands of the government. Turn the Federal Reserve into a Clearing House only must be the first order of business. Anything less is just a futile try to dislodge the pirates of Wall Street. The founders knowing the sleazy bankers wrote the Constitution to put control of the money in the hands of the government. Never to place it in disreputable private hands. It is written in article 1, section 8 of our Constitution.

Section. 8.

To coin Money, regulate the Value thereof, and of foreign Coin, and fix the Standard of Weights and Measures.

For centuries, the human strive have fought the tyrannical evil monarchies. They have bamboozled us into believing that all those evils are in the past. Nothing could be further from the truth. Physics teaches us that we do not destroy energy we can only transform it. The same thing can be said about the absolute monarchies. They have not been destroyed, only transformed into what we know today as banks. The Banks in today's world rule over us with the same iron first as the most ruthless and despicable kings or emperors of the past. They quench their thirst for blood by creating wars and famine. They break your backs by giving you more toils and taxing you to death. They control your education, information, the military, and religion. I insist, this history should have been accessible for Obama. Unless of course he already knows it. After all he has received brainwashing form Dr. Brzezinski. Remember? However, what rings the bell and perk your ears is the silent of mainstream media. The chairman of the Federal Reserve makes a comment of this importance. And not one journalist or politician raises eyebrows. This is what I call living in a sorry state of apathy and complacency. Let's face it. For decades, the education in America is under Zionist control. It's shaped to advance their purposes. We don't have freedom of press anymore. With few newspapers the Zionist have taken control the newspapers. The television networks serve for diversion as well as a deceiving tool. We are so used to that by now it's difficult to free those whose chains they have learned to revere or to love. Those who stand to lose, will oppose you, ridicule you, and attack you and destroy you if given the chance. Dr. Ray Hagin the African philosopher puts it this way: *"Those who control the printing page; control the thinking of the age."* So, we live in the world that Woodrow Wilson talked about one hundred years ago. This is what you call total domination if you have any doubts.

Woodrow Wilson became President by beating the incumbent William Howard Taft. He was the early favorite and by far more likable than Woodrow Wilson. He lost because he had vowed to veto any legislation trying to set up a central bank. This disqualified him as the banker's candidate of choice. Bernard Baruch, was a conspiring banker mogul of shady reputation and a Zionist. He brought Woodrow Wilson to the Democratic Party headquarters in 1912. Baruch like Dr. Brzezinski on Obama exercised his seductive power of persuasion on Wilson. What Baruch and his cronies wanted was the Central Bank and Wilson wanted the presidency to help the Zionist cause. Wilson despised the Constitution and our form of government. A terrible deal for America! Like a match made in Hell. Wilson sold his soul to the devils bankers of New York, in exchange for political and financial support. He received financial support from the Rockefeller, Morgan and indirectly from the Rothschild bankers. History records that Wilson swore in secret that if elected President, he would support the banker's Federal Reserve scam. Also, he would push for the first ever progressive income tax on the American people.

Now, it's hard to believe, but all this chain of events came to fruition in 1913. Wilson did not believe in the blessing of liberties as stipulated by the Constitution. He reveals his true colors in his erudite tome Constitutional Government in the United States (1908). When you start to understand Wilson's mind, then you can begin to feel it wasn't too hard for him to make a deal of this sheer size. Is no exaggeration. Baruch and his Zionists cronies were scientists, and unscrupulous. These Zionists had skills and knowledge so far above and beyond the average that would make a PhD like Wilson feel like and 8th grader. If you find this hard to believe, think what they did with Woodrow Wilson. He was a PhD in political science and knew little about foreign affairs. But the Zionist bankers did. They were so far ahead and had such a wealth of knowledge that they run circles on Wilson. So, to carry out their plans to elect Wilson J.P. Morgan and Rockefeller went on and played all sides of the election battlefield. Just like they do with the wars, they poured money into the candidacy of Teddy Roosevelt, even more than on Wilson and Taft. As a result, Roosevelt like an idiot played into their hands, and took away the votes Taft needed to win over Wilson. This election was the fundamental moment in history. The United States would become the worse ruled nation in the civilized world. Thank to Woodrow Wilson a huge victory for the Zionist.

We know little about Bernard Baruch aside his official biography. For the Zionist world. He is a philanthropist, statesman, political consultant, and presidential adviser to six presidents. Well, that's the official story; here is the rest of the story. On the day Bernard Baruch first introduced Woodrow Wilson to the wealthy Jewish community of New York. Baruch led Wilson around "as if he was a poodle on a string". You see. For the Zionist Wilson has been just a useful idiot. A tool to advance their world domination agenda. The essential reason is that Wilson liked to be part of the Zionist plans.

After the United States entered WWI. Baruch will lead the Wilson's War Industries Board. This profitable opportunity made him millions of dollars. Apart from becoming the most powerful figure in American industry. In his own words Bernard Baruch, testifying at a Congressional inquiry, said: *"I had more power than any other man in the war."*

Jonah Goldberg is an editor, a columnist and author. Describes Wilson as an imperialist, totalitarian warmonger. Who, from his youth, was "infatuated with political power" and then corrupted by it. After this you might think that this critic is going too far with his pungent points of view, but my grandmother used to say. "Tell me who you hang around with, and I tell you who you're." To be accurate, Woodrow Wilson chose poorly when he chose Zionists for friends. He lived at a time where prominent national leaders for the first time were open to criticizing the Constitution but Wilson wanted to do without it.

Ronald Pestritto the political scientist. In his book "Woodrow Wilson and the Roots of Modern Liberalism". Described in Woodrow Wilson's presidency. "Leadership in Wilson's administration was not as democratic as it seems. But instead amounts to elite governance under a veneer of democratic rhetoric". I supposed that makes Wilson a snob. Knowing that he was a southerner. Hanging around with the Jewish elite of New York like a puddle. Not exactly as an equal he must have resented that a little bit, but rather than sticking to his roots he runs the presidency like an elitist. Ronald Pestritto explains Wilson as the reformer, his thoughts about the Constitution. The document he swore to uphold and defend.

"Wilson contended that a system of government established in the late 1700s in a small, sparsely populated country had become inadequate in a world of industrialization, immigration, international tensions and other developments the founders couldn't have foreseen. The government therefore had to adapt."

What Wilson said is the country is getting bigger in population and is moving forward. Plus, the country is making more goods than ever as the modern industry advances. As a result, government must also grow bigger.

Are you for real Woody?

Wilson studied political science. Therefore, he must know what Thomas Jefferson said about big government. "When a government is big enough to give you everything. The government can also to take it away." Thanks to Woodrow Wilson that is the danger we live in today. Remember after 9/11 Congress had to trouble passing the Patriot Act in the name of protecting the people. But it did not consider restricting or removing our God given individual liberties. Wilson is a progressive, but his thoughts and ideas are of a good leftist. You know, the socialist, communist, Leninist, collectivist. Wilson dismissed the purpose the Constitution of the United States is to secure the blessing of Liberty. It does not give us the Liberty, it protects it. Big difference with the collectivism constitution. The Collectivist constitution around the world share one characteristic. They protect the group first the individual second. They provide rights and liberties to its citizens, and have the authority to take them away. Is ridiculous for Wilson to believe our Constitution is obsolete. The struggle, significance of the American Revolution is not for us Americans to forget. Today the American Revolution has greater significance than ever. Take a look at your paycheck and realize the Zionist noose on your neck is getting tighter than ever. Let me tell you. Until the American Revolution occurred. The whole world has lived more than 3000 years of tyranny, between monarchies, empires and the likes. It's only after the American Revolution that we have guaranteed, Individual Rights and Liberties. For the first time in history! In case you're missing the point it was unique, historically and revolutionary. Unlike the communist revolutions of the twentieth century seeking complete control of its citizens. You become property of the state. Just like the way of the old days of the Kings and Emperors. Therefore, the American Revolution became the road and path to individual rights and liberties. This is what makes it worth keeping, worth fighting for, worth preserving. The disappointing Wilson believed in the old curse and plague of slavery. The tyrannical ways of government we suffered since the beginning of humanity. The American Revolution was the historic event that gave us individual rights for the first time. Wilson wanted to do away with the American Revolution and the blessings of Liberty. Do you think he the wrong man to be our president? I mean a PhD in political science from Princeton should have known this stuff.

Perhaps his religious upbringing had something to do with it. In my humble opinion when you add southerner plus bible it equals racist. As a Presbyterian, perhaps his father read Martin Luther to young Woody. This early religious lecturing could have had horrendous results in the ethical beliefs of our future president. Martin Luther the former Augustinian monk was a teacher in theology, member of the German secret society the Rosicrucians. In 1517 Martin Luther posted his 95 complaints against the Catholic Church. He protested selling pardons to everybody who believe their scam. What people don't usually know is that he hated freethinking and freedom of expression. In one of his sermons he said to his followers.

"You should throw spit in the face of reason, because she was the devil's whore, rotten with the itch of leprosy, and should be kept in the toilet".

Way to Go Martin!!

No wonder he didn't end burned at the stake because this is the crap Popes like to hear anyway. He Added.

"Damned be love into the abyss of hell, if it's maintained to the damage of faith... It is better that tyrants should sin a hundred times against the people than the people should sin once against

the tyrants... the ass wants to be thrashed, the mob to be governed by force."

Funny the way this backward people made into history.

Who is his right mind would builds a whole church movement based on the ideas of this sick minded bastard! Martin Luther not founder material. Sorry if you are a Lutheran, but it's time to open your eyes. You had to be downright ignorant to follow this guy. Perhaps to support his rebellion Martin also had the financial support of the bankers. I don't know. It's possible for Woodrow Wilson to pick up on these teachings. His religious upbringing was strong and helped him to become the racist he was. This is Wilson's voice in his tome Constitutional Government in the United States (1908).

"Constitution was not meant to hold the government back to the time of horses and wagons"

He deplored the way the branches of government check-mated one another to stall progress or what he saw as the progress and admired the British parliamentary system as more efficient.

No wonder Jonah Goldberg's describes Wilson as an imperialist, totalitarian warmonger. When you consider this information and ideas. Do you still think Wilson is Nobel Peace prize material?

Consider this the next time you hear talking about Woodrow Wilson. This president raised his voice against the monopolies in the United States. Who already stated that we are governed by a small group of dominant men. Yet, he betrayed his progressive political beliefs, joined the New York Jewish Zionist Elite. He helped create the most destructive monopoly of them all the Federal Reserve System. Our hogwash history recalls creating the Federal Reserve is Wilson's greatest domestic achievement. But, if we let the truth escape. It's the greatest calamity, misfortune, tragedy, a blow the American government has ever taken. He condemned the American people to eternal Zionist servitude by the stroke of a pen. Good-bye Democracy, Republic, and Freedom. Hello Slavery, Servitude, and Collectivism. We have missed all this tragedy right under our noses. This should tell us the manipulating genius of the Zionist and their greatest triumph. So, please believe when I say freedom and democracy is just illusion. The branches of government are under Zionist control. That's a given. So now, they give us democracy like a master rations treats to his poppy, just a little to make us feel good every once in a while. In essence, Wilson betrayed the Constitution and betrayed his country. He does not deserve remembrance with glory and devotion. We should remember Wilson with scorn and indignation.

If we want to Identify the enemy we need to know who is a Zionist. And what do they stand for? First, we should know not all Jews are Zionist sympathizers and not all Zionists are Jews. For that, we have the Useful Idiot VP Joe Biden who proudly confessed. "I'm a Zionist" to Israeli television. The Zionist International Banker follows certain profile that we must be able to identify. To start stopping them in their tracks we must be able to expose them. The Zionist bankers are individuals that display keen objectivity to their goals. They stay focused, and they are from tip to toe immune to feeling of patriotism. They show a total indifference of the human condition. Now, the interesting part we must ask is: How did they get such state of mind? Well, they have developed a Master Plan. The following comes from the Zionist Master Plan for World Power Domination.

Let me point out. It's not the intent this book, to focus on the Jewish people but the individuals listed. So, here we go. Back in the 50's Russell Maguire owned the American Mercury Magazine. He was a wealthy and clever businessperson who expressed his opposition to the Zionist Jewish Agenda. One day at work in his office, a well-researched manuscript to be The Zionism's Master Plan for World Power dropped into his lap. After reading it and ponder on it, he decided to go ahead and make it public. Because of his courage. Maguire endured attempted blackmail, physical threat, and the complete sabotage of his business. Typical retaliation of those Zionist we cannot criticize. Because the Zionist cannot withstand criticism. Thus, the Maguire publication was like throwing holy water on a vampire. Thus, unable to bear criticism the Zionist retaliated. The French philosopher Voltaire said these simple and wise words of wisdom. "To learn who rules over you; find out whom you cannot criticize". And we know who we cannot criticize, don't we. So, to confirm this expose let me present a tiny excerpt of this Zionist Central document:

A Chronology of the Zionist Master Plan for World Domination:

This chronology compiles direct quotations from Zionists or from their books. At the end of each paragraph you find listed the books, their authors, the publishing firms and the dates of each publication. I. B. Means "International Banker," A. M. Means "American Mercury," p. Means "page," MMM means 'Money Made Mysterious."

1896

Theodor Herzl published "The Jewish State." It became the Zionists' bible. The following are the exact quotes are from Herzl's book:

1897

1. Lord Edmond Rothschild of London and Jacob H. Schiff of New York City, two of the Elders of Zion, got Theodor Herzl (of Austria) to arrange for the World Zionist Congress at Basel, Switzerland; 197 delegates met there and laid out a plan of World Conquest with plans for a World Government. Herzl, founder of Zionism, in opening the meeting, raised his right hand and repeated an ancient oath of the Talmudists:

"If I forget thee, O Jerusalem, may my right hand forget its cunning." Herzl also said at this meeting: "We are one nation. We are neither American nor Russian Jews, but only Jews!" He also said: 'With a few exceptions that do not figure at all, the entire press of the world is in our hands."

2. Dr. Mandelstam said on August 29 at the opening of the Zionist Congress of 1897: "The Jews will use all their influence and power to prevent the rise and prosperity of other nations and are resolved to adhere to their historic hopes; i.e., to the conquest of world power." LE TEMPS, Paris, September 3,1897.

3. The Zionist Organization of America organized in 1897 by Richard Gottheil of Columbia University as its first president, and Rabbi Stephen Wise as the first secretary. Branches for women (Hadassah), and children (Young Judea) were soon organized. ZIONIST NETWORK, p. 32.

I have bolded those phrases that I think are most significant for our purpose. We don't exaggerate if we think how important this document is to help us learn who the Zionist are. The Master Plan exposes the Zionist agenda of world domination more than any other document. I bring this up because you need to know what Bernard Baruch believed in and what he pretended to achieve. What his association with Woodrow Wilson meant to him and all his fellow Zionists. Pirates such as JP Morgan, John D. Rockefeller, Lord Edmond Rothschild of London and Jacob H. Schiff just to mention a few. Bernard Baruch was so certain the US would enter WWI that in 1915 while the US was still at peace. He took part of his annual income of $2,000,000 to finance training soldiers to fight in a war which Baruch said he knew was coming. AMERICAN MERCURY October, 1956, page Eighty-three

The official story is that World War I started after Archduke Franz Ferdinand murder. On June 28, 1914 by Gavrilo Princip a member of the secret Black Hand society. This was a nationalist movement favoring a union between Bosnia-Herzegovina and Serbia. This man, Gavrilo Princip was sick with tuberculosis and had little life left in him. So, it was a suicide mission perpetrated by this poor soul Gavrilo Princip. He was nothing but a poppet of the Zionist cartel. Now, perhaps you never thought about this before. Or your history teacher never brought this up. Are you going to tell me that this guy's death, the Archduke Franz Ferdinand was so important that he'd cause the whole world to go to war? I don't think so.

President John F. Kennedy was far more important. far wiser and more brave than this guy. But when they killed JFK in the middle of the cold war we didn't go to war. President Lyndon Johnson increased in size of the Vietnam war overnight, but we cannot say that was a world war. So; what's wrong with this picture? Do you remember President Eisenhower who warned us about the Military Complex?

Now here are the real reasons the Zionist caused WWI. It was the great nation of Germany in partnership with the Ottoman Empire disturbed the Zionist in England and the United States. Germany also started to build the Orient Express, yes the Berlin Bagdad Railroad. Reason behind was that by 1908 they discovered oil in Persia. Around this time the British Navy had changed from coal to oil as a fuel source and so did Germany. But Germany did not have any oil producing colonies, so it looked to the east; to the rich oil fields in Iraq, Iran, and Saudi Arabia. At the early part of the twentieth century this vast part of the world was part of the Ottoman Empire. This strategic move could have made Germany perhaps the most powerful nation in Europe. The Zionist would oppose this idea. The Anglo-American Establishment of Cecil Rhodes was already in force and were not about to let Germany control the Middle-East. So, they designed to assassinate this poor devil the Archduke Ferdinand and got us all into war. Killing millions of innocent people on both sides only to satisfy the Zionist thirst for blood and power.

Meanwhile, President Wilson appointed the first Zionist Jew to serve on the Supreme Court Justice Louis Brandeis. He was one of President Wilson's friends and closest adviser. Still, how did he get the nomination to the Supreme Court? This is what you call cashing in old favors. It turned out that President Wilson entangled himself in some "moral problems". At Princeton University Wilson met a charming divorcee Mrs. Mary Peck. So the story ran that in his earlier days Brandeis saved the future President from appearing in a damaging lawsuit. In the end Wilson regarded Brandeis as the man to whom he owed his career. So, why not return the favor and make Brandeis Chief Justice. Brandeis did such a fine job that Mrs. Mary Peck never press any charges and Woodrow Wilson never paid hush money or blackmail. Another close associate of Woodrow Wilson was Colonel Edward Mandell House. This was an honorary rank because he never served in the army. But he was much on active duty serving for the Zionist Rothschild and Jacob Schiff. Colonel House preyed on his wicked connections to become the hidden power behind Wilson. He became so close to Wilson that he even had living quarters in the White House. You can say that he lived-in the White House free and clear, while exerting enormous influence to the president.

Way to go Eddy! Live off the taxpayer's money. That's the Zionist way.

After signing Federal Reserve Jacob Schiff sent Colonel House a letter thanking him for his important role and for a job well done. In Woodrow Wilson's personal journal we found this letter written by Colonel House Vader. He says to Wilson.

"Very soon, every American will be required to register their biological property (that's you and your children) in a national system designed to keep track of the people and that will operate under the ancient system of pledging. By such methodology, we can compel people to submit to our agenda, which will affect our

security as a charge back for our fiat paper currency. Every American will be forced to register or suffer being able to work and earn a living. They will be our chattels (property) and we will hold the security interest over them forever, by operation of the law merchant under the scheme of secured transactions. Americans, by unknowingly or unwittingly delivering the bills of lading (Birth Certificate) to us will be rendered bankrupt and insolvent, secured by their pledges. They will be stripped of their rights and given a commercial value designed to make us a profit and they will be none the wiser, for not one man in a million could ever figure our plans and, if by accident one or two should figure it out, we have in our arsenal plausible deniability. After all, this is the only logical way to fund government, by floating liens and debts to the registrants in the form of benefits and privileges. This will inevitably reap us huge profits beyond our wildest expectations and leave every American a contributor to this fraud, which we will call "Social Insurance." Without realizing it, every American will unknowingly be our servant, however begrudgingly. The people will become helpless and without any hope for their redemption and we will employ the high office (presidency) of our dummy corporation (USA) to foment this plot against America."

If this isn't the smoking gun I don't know what is!!

Thomas Jefferson once said: Eternal Vigilance is the price of Liberty. We have not done our job. We have fumbled the ball and the Zionists have scored big time. Still, this game is not over. Not until we exhaust all our strength to oppose them. We can recover our loses and we can still win. We need to learn their strategies and beat them at their own game. Long Live the Fighters!

Since creating the Fraudulent Reserve. We have incurred into trillions and trillions of dollars in debt. We have lost millions and millions of lives in un-warranted wars. All this catastrophes to satisfy the Zionist greed and thirst for power. It's time to clip the wings of these vampires.

Chapter 3

There Were Many Signs

Many prominent men have spoken, and have tried to expose these power hungry Zionists with little success. They have tried to enlighten us with a trail of sings they left behind, but still unsuccessful. I can only hope this material falls in the hands of millions of people living in oblivion. I believe the Internet is the best weapon we have. It's a double edge sword and we need to use for our advantage. Connecting the dots of our hidden history is what we need to start doing and what is going to open our eyes. Without this knowledge we will continue seeing signs on the wall, but we will fall on the trap because we don't know how to read them. We need to start by asking the right questions to our elected officials. If we find out they are under Zionist control expose them and kick them out of office. The Zionist madness has to stop. The only way we can do that is by checking your local Zionists and crush their plans. More than 2000 years ago Plato wrote:

"One of the penalties for refusing to participate in politics is that you end up being governed by your inferiors." And in another quote he also said: "The price good men pay for indifference to public affairs is to be ruled by evil men."

We have no doubt on this one. This is our case, unfortunately.

The conventional historians consider Woodrow Wilson our PhD President an intellectual. That means a person with vast knowledge and wisdom. Just a few decades before Wilson's time there have been terrible deeds committed against President Jackson. Old Hickory dared not to renew bankers charter. Thus, Jackson had to endure the full wrath of the International Bankers. Wilson is accountable for not considering these facts. Since the beginning of the Republic from the times of Alexander Hamilton, Andrew Jackson, and Abraham Lincoln. The International bankers wanted to install their despicable Central Bank in America. It's not possible that Wilson never learned about the ordeals. The troubles President Andrew Jackson had to go through to keep the central bank away. Jackson risked his live to keep us free from this nest of vipers as he called them. Andrew Jackson, the seventh president of the United States, armed with courage and without fear, had this to say to a delegation of international bankers in 1832.

"Gentlemen, I have had men watching you for a long time, and I am convinced that you have used the funds of the bank to speculate in the breadstuffs of the country. When you won, you divided the profits among you, and when you lost, you charged it to the bank. You tell me that if I take the deposits from the bank and annul its charter, I shall ruin ten thousand families. That may be true, gentlemen, but that is your sin! Should I let you go on, you will ruin fifty thousand families, and that would be my sin! You are a den of vipers and thieves. I intend to rout you out, and by the eternal God, I will rout you out."

How can you miss this Wilson? This historic quote already was available at the time he was a student at Princeton. In fact, with a little effort, he could have found a survivor to tell him the story. Firsthand! Had Wilson taken heed of these words. Maybe, just maybe he would have seen what a wolf in sheep's clothing Baruch and Colonel House were. Wilson might have stopped their wicked plans. Any student of political science should have learned this important little piece of history. Just stop for a moment. Relax, take a deep breath. Read it carefully, you can see what the bankers did to Jackson are doing today accurately and with impunity. What we will discover is the template for the 2008 crisis; only this time, a hundred times bigger. Just like the atomic bombs dropped in Japan, those were mini-bombs if you compare to the ones they can drop today. Once again, the 2008 debacle was another demonstration the bankers can create a worldwide financial crisis, and no one is safe. Nobody pointed the finger at them and nobody went to jail. They have done a great job at keeping the public at below the stupid level. While their NWO (New World Order) plans continue uninterrupted, unchallenged, and with impunity.

Meanwhile, what can we say about our graduated students on Economics? Are they getting the real scoop? Is their teacher teaching them about the fraudulent banking industry? I've heard a graduated student saying the economy of today is a lot different from the economy of the past. That might be true if you apply today's technology. However, building a healthy economy based on lies and deceit is never a good idea and is doom to collapse. From the beginning the Federal Reserve assumed control of the money supply and this has proven disastrous. Why do you think the US dollar is worth less and less every year? Inflation you say. Well, where is the economic stability the Federal Reserve promised us. One of the strongest arguments to create the Federal Reserve was to provide economic stability. Here too the Federal Reserve has failed miserable. A hallmark of a stable economy is to keep Inflation at bay. Another objective the Federal Reserve have failed. From Physics let us consider money as matter. Inflation is so destructive that you can call it antimatter. Inflation eats our savings and the value of our assets like a cancer. Still, we much misunderstand Inflation just like cancer. Inflation comes to us in the form of a tax. Why do I say that inflation is a tax? We will try to show with a simple explanation the complex idea of inflation. Since Congresthes can borrow an indiscriminate amount of money from the Federal Reserve the money supply has increased out of control. Every expense the Federal Government incurs the Federal Reserve records it as debt. As a result, that fraudulent debt the Federal government passes it to the taxpayer as tax. This is why taxes rise and we see more taxes every year. Prices rise, we call it inflation, but is taxation without representation or without saying so, you might say. That's where we are. This is the tyranny we live-in If you think we live in a democracy think again. As long as the government keeps taxing you without your knowledge, your democracy is a joke. For any conscious politician would realize we're not qualified to campaign abroad waiving the flag of freedom and democracy. We're making a total joke of ourselves We should fix our problems here first. Until then, we don't have the moral right to bring democracy and freedom to other countries.

The Federal Reserve with omnipotent status and without supervision has loaned to the Government an unknown amount of money. This Federal Reserve no one can thoroughly audit has printed money on its own and loaned it to other governments, and companies that we don't know about. They designed the scam for the government to pick up the tab when the loan defaults. As a result is the taxpayer that ends paying that bad loan. The Bank never loses. Increasing the debt ceiling only causes more debt that in the end reflects in all the taxes that we pay. So there you have it, in just a few words how inflation erodes your saving, buying power, and why is a tax. Another example of the banker's unfair games. It's time to go back to our main business.

I suppose Woodrow Wilson never read about Nicholas Biddle. When Andrew Jackson was President; Biddle was the general manager of the 2nd Bank of the United States. When President Jackson refused to renew his charter this is what Biddle said:

"Nothing but widespread suffering will produce any effect on congress... Our only safety is in pursuing a steady course of firm monetary restriction – and have no doubt that such a course will ultimately lead a restoration of the currency and re-charter of the bank." Nicholas Biddle; 1832.

Can you see the extortion, force, blackmail, in Biddle's words? And to make sure that his intents were sincere, he carried out his threat by restricting the money supply. Biddle single-handed caused serious economic instability aimed to undermine Jackson's supporters. It's not prudent to let one man or a few men control the power of money. What do you think?

Nicholas Biddle, Alan Greenspan, and Ben Bernanke. They have cultivated the idea the banker is above government and above the law like if they walk on water. They believe that only they are good enough to exercise self-discipline and to self-regulate. They really believe all this hogwash, but we don't have to believe this crap because we know better. Looking through centuries of banking history, they have proved the contrary. It's our fault we have not taken them to court and thrown in jail. It's our fault we have not recovered the power of money and put it under government control. The Zionist Bankers think they are the cardinal of the economic temple. The Catholic Church through a grave error gave its cardinals powers far beyond their capacity to manage. These powers proved too great for them to realize. Their lust for power and control were stronger than doing right by God. Throughout history the church has displayed a long list of despicable crimes and conspiracies. If the so called holy men of God betrayed the church. Why would we think the disreputable bankers are any different? The bankers have betrayed. They drive their insatiable thirst for money and power. I like to point out that Nicholas Biddle was one smart individual. He graduated from the University of Pennsylvania at the tender age of thirteen. Early on in his life he entered the banking and financial business of the elite. He traveled to Europe to become a great asset of the International Bankers Circle. We can say the same about Benjamin Bernanke. Although he didn't graduate early in his life like Biddle, he graduated from the prestigious Massachusetts Institute of Technology. Bear in mind that Zionist look for the brightest, and the smartest. Those with signs of weakness, they will subject to seduction, programming, and indoctrination. That's how, their collaborators train to serve willingly for their Master's goals. But where was Woodrow Wilson that he didn't take note of these facts, why didn't he react and stop and ponder for a moment. For a capable President with integrity, should have known they Zionist were getting ready to unleash an highly elaborated conspiracy. A masterful sting laced with deception, intrigue, ill-will, malice and above all panic and fear.

We need to remember that in 1907 JP Morgan started what we remember as the panic of 1907. With that maneuver he made the public ripe to cry for banking reform. Let's not forget that JP Morgan was an agent of the Rothschild Zionist family. He sat among those 7 members of the Jekyll Island secret meeting in November 1910. A report said that when he died, only 15% of his wealth belonged to him, the rest was all Rothschild property. Have you heard of JP Morgan Chase? Who do you think that bank belongs to?

The problem we have with Woodrow Wilson is his hidden political, and religious beliefs. He was unfaithful to the heart values the US Constitution. In his mind he was more willing to sell out to the Zionist believing he would secure America and the rest of world for democracy.

What a lofty idea! We're screwed.

Are you willing to accept that he never read Patrick Henry. Despite all his years of education and vast experience and expertise? Patrick Henry, a fellow Virginian said this about the Constitution.

"The Constitution is not an instrument for the government to restrain the people, it is an instrument for the people to restrain the government – lest it comes to dominate our lives and interest."

This is a deep, wonderful and revolutionary idea that puts Patrick Henry in a unique place in our history. Patrick Henry is among those people who carved the history that defines us as Americans. We should honor Patrick Henry remembering his words to preserve and uphold the blessing of liberty. The Federal Reserve would have never been possible if the politicians would have remembered Patrick Henry.

We need to understand and, until the American Revolution. The whole world belonged to the tyrannical governments and monarchies around the planet. They used and misused their authority like the emperor Constantine to set of laws to restrain and control the masses. We change that, for the first time in human history, and that was nothing but revolutionary. Rest assured the American Revolution is unique there has never been another revolution aimed to defend the rights of the individual. For Woodrow Wilson not considering the wisdom of Patrick Henry is short of betrayal. I think is downright sinful, and seditious. As the president of the United States, Woodrow Wilson is under the duty to take guidance on the values America stands for. Rather than acting like a true American President. He preferred to follow his delusion of grandeur. Wilson went the opposite direction and helped the Zionist gain control of the most important part of our freedom. The Money Power. But his biographers are happy to rationalize the gravity of his crime. They omit this important event because they have their careers and reputations to preserve. Because nothing escapes the controlled press. Their books have to pass reviewed for content before they go into printing. For us only few publishers remain not under Zionist control. The majority control the press and it is they who control the printed page. As a result, they control your thinking. That's why we can never get the truth from the standard media channels. We must get it from outside the grid if we want to start thinking for ourselves. Give up the cable and satellite will you?

This is another magnificent quote from President Andrew Jackson we should heed:

"If congress has the right under the Constitution to issue paper money, it was given them to use themselves, not to be delegated to individuals or corporations." -Andrew Jackson

Here is President Andrew Jackson quoting the Constitution in regards of issuing the money. I mean come on Woodrow this is the law of the land. I mean you and your PhD never heard that before! You know Andrew Jackson was not a PhD or anything like that, maybe he wasn't as refined and cultivated as Woodrow Wilson. Still Jackson refused to become a banker's poppet he had a clear idea what these bankers, these vitriol vultures were all about. Now, if I go back to the days of Woodrow Wilson and I don't know anything about banking. Like Obama, Clinton or Busch. But I if am presented with this piece of banking legislation I think I should have done my own research. Then, and after careful examination of this short but powerful statement from an ex-president of the United States I think I would have wanted to go back and examined the results of Jackson's actions. Then, and after a conscientious fact-finding of President Jackson actions. It would lead me to the conclusion the country's economy did well during those years. In fact, after President Jackson killed the bank as he said it. As a result, he paid all the government debts, and managed to balance the budget. Not bad for a hillbilly President!! Now, when was the last time we heard a president has balanced the budget!! Nonetheless, with this evidence and historical facts Wilson decided to cooperate, to join, to conspire with the Zionist. The vultures that just a few decades ago, his predecessor Andrew Jackson blatantly rejected.

It's obvious, Wilson here allowed the turtle to escape. You have to be so obtuse to let something like this happen right before your eyes. He had his head buried in the sand so deep, that he let his streak of stubbornness take the better of him. On the other hand, Wilson could have been in love or too busy writing love letters to that cute divorce of his Mrs. Mary Peck. Except that happened in

Princeton however, a President should know better than to allow the Zionists manipulation treat him like a puppy.

I hope you can understand how important it is to know our history from none Zionist sources. As we continue a different picture will emerge from what you have seen before. Discovering the rest of the story this what we should do if we want to oppose the Zionist. The tough reality is the people you cannot trust are those you cannot criticize. It's urgent to know the Zionist as a group and individuals. They are working against us, and we need to hinder their movements and not just watch the news in complacency. Know that is about time to become more prepare educated citizen and worthy opponent. So far the Zionist have had an easy time advancing their agenda of world domination. I think it's time to start changing that a little bit. Remember; it takes ten thousand trees to build a whole town, but it only takes one match to burn the whole forest.

When I think of poor President Obama, he's just another gofer, another servant of the Zionists. He just watches what happens around him and then; he wonders what happened. Since his presidential decisions are not his own. He doesn't have the balls to reduce the Zionist presence in his administration. I mean, how could he? They helped to put him in office. Remember his advertisement manager David Axelrod. His economic adviser, and financial supporter, Chicago billionaire Penny Pritzker. And the Chicago leftist activist (collectivist) and special adviser Valerie Jarrett. Doesn't strike you strange the closest advisers to President Obama are all Zionist Jews? It's because of this unfair advantage the Zionist have the Palestinians stand no change at getting a fair treatment. Worse still the chances to incur in abuses against the Palestinians are too great. Bet that all these advisers are members of the AIPAC (American Israel Public Affairs Committee). Which by the way it's the most powerful of the entire lobbyist groups that control the US Congress.

At the State Department. Most of members that control the section of foreign affairs of the middle east are all Zionist Jews. No wonder our foreign policies are so harmful for the Palestinians and so favorable to Israel. Look up the State Department website yourself, check their names.

Have you noticed Obama has aged a lot in these last six years. I guess it's not all fun and games. Our President is a CIA agent and a CFR collaborator. I am sorry to burst your bubble but both organizations, are under foreign control and work for foreign interest. What must weigh on him is to feel surrounded by Zionist just to do their bidding and powerless to do the right thing for America. In Woodrow Wilson's case, he had a choice and he had it in his hands to keep our nation free. Andrew Jackson unlike Wilson, did not yield and kept the bankers from controlling our currency. Abraham Lincoln used the Constitution to print the greenbacks. That's how he financed the Civil War and tried to keep the union intact. I say tried because the Union never was the same after the Civil War.

If Wilson never heard or learned what Andrew Jackson did during his presidency, maybe because it was too long ago. How about President Lincoln? Wilson grew up seeing the scars the Civil War left in America. The period of recovery, and the causes and effects, abolishing slavery which marked our nation forever. Wilson has no excuse if he didn't know what President Lincoln had to say about money:

"The Government should create, issue, and circulate all the currency and credits needed to satisfy the spending power of the Government and the buying power of consumers. By the adoption of these principles, the taxpayers will be saved immense sums of interest. Money will cease to be master and become the servant of humanity." Abraham Lincoln.

Lincoln clearly understood whoever controls the money is the master and the rest are just the servants. For Wilson, after learning what Andrew Jackson did to keep America free and advised to continue to do so. What's more, Abraham Lincoln description to make money the servant of humanity and not the other way around. What would you do in the Oval Office with a bill for creating a private central bank? I mean, armed with this knowledge and wisdom, would you act so recklessly? Would you do it in good conscience? Of course not! Not if you want to put America first. But why then, why Woodrow Wilson did sign us into slavery. For those biographers who don't want to tell the story. It should shock you to know that Wilson despised the constitution. He despised the idea of the checks and balances between the branches of government. The foundation of our government. Wilson based his ideas on believing the Constitution was already obsolete. A piece of paper, archaic for Wilson's time.

Talked about a self-important prick. Wilson the warmonger, racist, egomaniac prick dared to go above and beyond the wisdom of the Constitution. He believed his thoughts and ideas were aloft the founding fathers when they wrote the constitution. The insolent prick! Would you have voted for him if you knew what his real attitude was? I wouldn't. At this point, he had to disguise his true ideas to the voters who supported his candidacy. Had the people been aware of Wilson's deception they wouldn't have gone for it. Sadly for us that didn't happen. The campaign strategy the Zionists devised for Wilson and it's execution was perfect. The results it yielded were far greater than their wildest expectations. Woodrow Wilson played a flawless role. Whitewashing the Constitution caused the lost of our freedom and gave slavery a new face. "Equal Opportunity".

The honorable Sandra Day O'Connor (CFR) and former chief Justice of the Supreme Court When asked "Why is the Constitution so important?" put it this way:

"What makes the Constitution worthy of our commitment? First and foremost, the answer is our freedom. It is, quite simply, the most powerful vision of freedom ever expressed. It's also the world's shortest and oldest national constitution, neither so rigid as to be stifling, nor so malleable as to be devoid of meaning."

"Our Constitution has been an inspiration that changed the trajectory of world history for the perpetual benefit of mankind. In 1787, no country in the world had ever allowed its citizens to select their own form of government, much less to select a democratic government. What was revolutionary when it was written, and what continues to inspire the world today, is that the Constitution put governance in the hands of the people."

You'll get no argument from me Sandra if what we want is to preserve this Constitution to live a life in freedom. Her statement goes much with Patrick Henry. "Liberty is not a fad or a thing of the past." In spirit, Liberty is the Holy Grail we humans have wanted and always fought for. Wilson didn't see it that way though.

I think it's safe to call Wilson a misfit from now on. Woodrow Wilson should have never become president, and that's why he became president of the Zionist. But he is not alone; recent examples of misfits are George W. Busch, what a moron. Bill Clinton, what a demagogue, opportunist, lying sack, all Zionist puppets. Here is a little piece on Bill Clinton and what he did to defend his Zionist masters. Representative Henry Gonzalez of Texas. The head of the House Banking Committee called in 1993 for an independent audit of the Federal Reserve. Bill Clinton being the ferret with the nose of a whistle expressed his concern this way:

"It would run the risk of undermining market confidence in the Fed." *"And, market confidence is what this fact comes down to. And one of the most potentially disastrous situations facing the United States."*

Is Billy a son of the U know what States or what!

Clinton, knows without a glitch the FED is nothing but a bunch of white-collar crooks. Rather than face the facts he preferred to uphold the lies in favor to his Zionist masters. Yes, the Federal Reserve could create potentially disastrous conditions. Just like in 1929 or what Nicholas Biddle did with President Jackson, but is nothing that we couldn't overcome. More important, these Zionists bastards could be out in the open if Clinton had paid attention to Henry Gonzales proposal. But if we were vigilant, prone to connect the dots. We could realize Clinton was telling us who his bosses are and we shouldn't mess with them. This presidential behavior leaves no doubt that Clinton is a double agent and he sold out to the Zionist. Which incidentally the Zionists are technically a foreign power.

How about the lion king Barrack Obama. Here you have the politician apprentice, an amateur in the political arena. Obama was an unprepared young whelp with almost no political achievements in the senate. There are no important or outstanding achievements that Obama can speak of. Still, he makes it to the Presidency? Obama for president was as rare event as finding a yellow dog. It's no secret the Zionist bankers helped Woodrow Wilson to the White House. It's also no secret that Barrack Obama received big contributions from the same Zionist bankers of today. History repeats itself. Those who pull the strings are working against us. They are winning so far, and as long as we remain sluggish and keep from connecting the dots they will keep on winning. I hope you can make it through the book and see how important is to know your history behind the history.

Every day we wake up the Zionists treat us like cattle. Oh yes!.. You might say. But I have freedom of speech, I am free to go anywhere, to do anything! So is the cow who is free to roam, eat and defecates wherever she pleases right? As long as she remains inside the fence, she is all right. However, the good news is that people like Joe Biden, George W. Busch, Bill Clinton, and Barrack Obama share on this fence. It makes no difference what degree you may have or what university you come from. As long as you remain within the circle of knowledge they define for you. As long as you know only what they want you to know, you'll be fine. But the moment you start thinking outside your circle of confinement or trying to get your head out the sand. You stop being a sheep, to turn into an annoyance to them. They might even consider you dangerous. Remember President Lincoln and President Kennedy. Both decided to use the Constitution and printed money interest free in favor of the people of the United States. Lincoln printed the greenback and President Kennedy issue EO11110 on May 1963. This order would give the Department of the Treasury authority to print money interest free. Well, what do you know? That's money we don't have pay taxes on. On November 1963 President Kennedy was murdered by the people who stood to lose the most. That's not a coincidence, Is it? They assassinated both Presidents because they dared to cross the International Bankers path.

So far, we have been talking about Wilson and what he knew and what he did. Now, it's time to introduce hard evidence to understand that Wilson knew exactly what he was doing. More important, he wanted to do it. Baruch and his Zionists cronies couldn't have asked for a better allied than Wilson. From the start, Wilson proved he was the man the Zionist were looking for. It's alarming to know that Wilson knew the ordeals President Jackson went through to fight the bankers. In fact, Wilson was a historian, and he wrote about President Jackson the following.

"General Jackson had come in "to simplify and purify the workings of the government, and to carry it back to the times of Mr. Jefferson, to promote its economy and efficiency, and to maintain the rights of the people and of the States in its administration"; and from the outset, with something of the instinct of the

communities in which he had been bred, he looked upon the Bank as an enemy of constitutional and democratic government. His attack upon it, begun in his first inaugural address, had been continued in every annual message he sent to Congress. He had begun by plainly intimating a doubt as to the legality of its institution, the Supreme Court to the contrary notwithstanding; and had asserted that it had failed to establish a stable currency. He next pronounced it an "un American monopoly." Finally, he expressed serious misgivings as to the soundness of its management. At each mention of it his warmth sensibly increased; his hostility became more open and aggressive. The purpose apparently grew upon him to destroy it. He forced it to meet him, as challengers, and fight for its life in the open field of politics". From the Lehrman Institute of American history.

It's clear that Wilson knew well that President Jackson had no love for the Bankers and with good reason. Something that Wilson dismissed, but it appears that Wilson makes these comments with a slight hint of mockery to Jackson's ideas. For instance.

"Simplify and purify the workings of the government and carry back to the times of Thomas Jefferson"

It means that President Jackson wanted to keep a small government as the founders thought it should be. As Patrick Henry said.

"The Constitution is not an instrument for the government to restrain the people, it's an instrument for the people to restrain the government- lest it come to dominate our lives an interest."

But for Wilson these words didn't mean anything. When Jackson called the Central Bank the Un-American Monopoly. Wilson reacts in disagreement. I mean, how dare he! Then again let us remember. What was Wilson trying to say during his campaigning for the presidency? Remember his speech?

"We have not one or two or three, but many, established and formidable monopolies in the United States. We have, not one or two, but many, fields of endeavor into which it is difficult, if not impossible, for the independent man to enter. We have restricted credit, we have restricted opportunity, we have controlled development, and we have come to be one of the worst ruled, one of the most completely controlled and dominated, governments in the civilized world — no longer a government by the opinion and the duress of small groups of dominant men."

While Wilson approved the bank monopoly Jackson was fighting against it. Wilson opposed the already well-known monopolies of his time. He cried out loud the monopolies are responsible when he said:

"We have come to be one of the worst ruled, one of the most completely controlled and dominated, governments in the civilized world."

Is he missing anything here?

These are alarming words Woody. Tell me then, for the love of God Woody why would you think the money monopoly would be any different? When what they have done well is present themselves as a menace, you know... Wolves in sheep's clothing. This is an enormous contradiction overlooked by Wilson biographers. Still, you find this contradiction often enough amount politicians of the worst kind. I mean. Like. Bill and Hillary Clinton. What a laying sacks they are. Please look-up a great movie dedicated to the American Queen of laying and deceit. Queen Hillary; her laying and contradictions, clip by clip in her own words. George W. Busch, he was the king's son, but what a buffoon. These people receive tutoring to become opportunist and sociopaths who would use whatever inroads they can make to lie and deceive to get what they want. Woodrow Wilson was no exception. Had he been alive during President Jackson's time, he would have opposed him and sided with Nicholas

Biddle. As he campaigned Wilson as a demagogue expressed his opposition against the monopolies, but he was ready to sign us up for the biggest and most dangerous of them all. In his heart and in his mind, he wanted to create the Federal Reserve Thus, creating a nation of slaves at the hands of the Zionist bankers with the stroke of a pen.

If you want to know how dangerous the Federal Reserve has proven to be. Well... There is profusion of evidence pointing to the Federal Reserve involving in every war since 1913. It's just undeniable the Zionist Banking Cartel had a lot to do with all the economic debacles we have suffered. The Federal Reserve crimes have left its fingerprints all over.

The pages of Woodrow Wilson's history is shocking at best. Because Wilson knew the history behind the Second Bank of the US and knew who Nicholas Biddle was. Let us see what Woodrow Wilson stood for before he signed the Federal Reserve into law. Just one more piece of evidence to shed more light into so we can forget about his feeling of remorse. This comes from the Lehrman Institute of American History.

"Economic historian Bray Hammond wrote that Biddle was a devoted, conscientious, and exceptionally able manager of the Central Bank up to the time the President and his advisers decided to do away with her and him too." Andrew Burstein noted: "The Bank of the United States was perfectly well managed. It regulated the availability of credit through its practical control over the loan activities of state banks. But to Jackson, the national bank was a morally suspect institution, a symbol of secret manipulation." Taking a more critical position, Arthur Schlesinger, Jr., argued: "Biddle not only suppressed all internal dissent but insisted flatly that the Bank was not accountable to the government or the people." Schlesinger wrote: "In Biddle's eyes the bank was...an independent corporation, on a level with the state, and not responsible to it except as the narrowest interpretation of the charter compelled. Biddle tried to strengthen this position by flourishing a theory that the bank was beyond political good or evil. That was anathema to Jackson. The Central Bank represented to Jackson the power of the unaccountable elite. Nevertheless, it did more for the economy than Jackson recognized." From the Lehrman Institute of American history.

First, let us understand Wilson's motivation is the content you have read above before and during his presidency at the White House. Let us take it one step at the time to analyze what all this means and see what it yields. Nicholas Biddle was a great bank manager. Intelligent and bright man, a true scholar in banking business. No doubt about Biddle's ability, but can we tell for whom he worked for? Knowing the Central Bank was a private corporation. It's safe to think that his first and chief concern was to produce profits for his shareholders. Further, he would do anything and everything in his power to keep and keep his shareholders happy. Not the American people, but the elite he served. This is what President Jackson understood and fought to preserve a government dedicated to serve the American people. Jackson did not trust the bankers and he had a good reason for it. He battled the Indians and killed thousands of them, a shameful deed that tainted his reputation forever. But he saw a greater and more insidious enemy in the bankers. Jackson was a military man. So as a good military man, Jackson studied another great military man in the name of Napoleon Bonaparte. The great French strategist suffered the clutches of the international bankers at the time he ruled France. Napoleon knew what a despicable bunch of bloodsuckers these bankers were. He left us with this warning.

"When a government is dependent upon bankers for money, they and not the leaders of the government control the situation, since the hand that gives is above the hand that takes... Money has no motherland; financiers are without patriotism and without decency;

their sole object is gain." – Napoleon Bonaparte, Emperor of France, 1815

These are significant and reveling words spoken by an important and brilliant man in his own right. Napoleon showed unique and exceptional skills in the battlefield and administration of government. While Nicholas Biddle displayed exceptional skills scamming banker. At Waterloo, Napoleon was double crossed by the Rothschild who financed both sides of the war. The term double cross you can see it symbolized in the Exxon logo. Exxon is part of the Zionist David Rockefeller conglomerate. As a result, in London the astute but shameful Nathan Rothschild received knowledge of the result in Waterloo 24 hours ahead that England have won the battle. He took advantage of this information and bought out the entire English debt for pennies on the pound. These maneuvers gave the Rothschild control of the English economy up to these days. Why dismiss all this important history? Should we overlook these decisive and instrumental events? What makes the bankers, so special? Why must we surrender whatever little rights and liberties we have left for their benefit? Fortunately, what works against them is there is plenty historical evidence to prove their deceitful practices.

What would set a part Andrew Jackson from Woodrow Wilson? Well, we can say with much certainty Jackson chose to heed Napoleon's words and Wilson dismissed it. For this, Wilson was grossly irresponsible and negligent to say the least.

Conventional historians speak well of Nicholas Biddle like if he was some messiah. Nick with the power to bring economic prosperity, and stability to the country. Our gratitude towards him should be like a God given present to humankind. Nick Biddle the boy wonder bought into that very well, he ran the bank like his little kingdom and he was the prince. More pretentious and pompous he couldn't have been. More important today Biddle's beliefs about his beloved bank have endured time. Today, Biddle's influence is present in the

Federal Reserve chairpersons Greenspan, Bernanke, Geithner. The present chairwoman Mrs. Janet Yellen. They have the conviction the Federal Reserve is a corporation accountable to no one. The Federal Reserve is not answerable to the federal government, Congress or the people of the United States. And you believed no one is above the law in The United States of America. Wrong!

We must remember. Biddle not only suppressed all internal dissent. His unyielding view said the Bank was not accountable to the government or the people." Can you believe the balls of this guy? How can a brilliant man born and raised in America the free would think such absurdity? America is where we believe no one is above the law. Leave it to the Zionists bankers and their shenanigans to create the disgusting Federal Reserve. If you don't hear too much protesting is because we are induce to live in lackluster. We are induce to live in indifference, utter submission and defeat. We are encourage to just let it continue as the natural order of things.

Don't say I didn't warn you!

Here in America thanks to Woodrow Wilson we have the Federal Reserve System a private corporation. A Banking Cartel running with the understanding is not accountable to the president, the Federal government. The Federal Reserve acts based on these rules from the start and no one, and I mean no one has been able to challenge it with any success. Biddle tried to push the theory the Central Bank was beyond political good or evil.

I mean; are you serious Biddle?

The reference the bible makes for these money changers is about Jesus whipping ass outside the temple. Biddle and his cronies are the same scammers Jesus whipped and for a good reason. Remember when the money changers tried to corner the market at the temple? Biddle, a brilliant and self-centered pompous ass had this believe. Ready for this: he believed the right to control the money supply descended from the grace of God. Thus, he didn't have to answer to no one. Like a supreme ruler Biddle thought the people had no right to question his divine right to command the awesome power of money.

Are you for real Nick?

Now I feel like smacking this guy around in the name of the people. But this is the way the boys from Wall Street feel and act today. If you wish to think otherwise you are deluding yourself.

Nick, have you ever heard that power corrupts and absolute power corrupts absolutely? No? You must think you're above those carnal temptations too. Biddle you're a banker, which means that you would give away umbrellas in a clear day, but you would take them away in a rainy day. The same allegory applies to present Federal Reserve and Zionist jokers. Greenspan, Bernanke, Paulsen, Geithner, and Janet Yellen. Why aren't these gurus of the financial world overtly involved in politics? Is because it doesn't matter to them who wins as long they keep their monopoly of money intact. But, rest assured that covertly. They are all over Congress buying political clout and influence whenever it suits them. It's hard to understand the insolence that Biddle and his successors have displayed until now. As it's hard to accept the Zionist have lied to us for so long. To think that they believe the government is beneath them. That they are accountable to no one is upholding, shocking, and unacceptable. The banking business idea was an iniquity conception of a sinful birth. That's why it has earned the worst reputation throughout history. To explain even further, here is a reference from President James Madison:

"History records the money changers have used every form of abuse, intrigue, deceit, and violent means possible to maintain their control over governments by controlling money and its issuance."- James Madison.

I don't think you can it explain clearer than that!

For James Madison knowing his history couldn't be more eloquent and more truthful than when he wrote those words. So, if Madison understood his history, so would Mr. PhD Wilson. There is only one way to answer that. Wilson thought like an elitist, and believed in the elitist cause. He thought of himself an elitist. Despite his modest lineage Wilson was seduced by the elite evil Zionists and the insatiable lust for power, run through his veins like an intoxicating venom. We can see it clearly in this extract of an essay he wrote about Andrew Jackson:

"The folly of staking the fortunes of the Bank against the popularity of General Jackson at the polls was quickly enough demonstrated. It was much easier for the mass of men who now held the votes in the country to believe the Bank a dangerous and corrupt monopoly than to understand the arguments of statesmen who argued of its services to the government and to commerce. They recognized General Jackson as a man of their own instincts, and deemed those instincts a sure enough guide in politics. Statesmen might approve of the Bank, but the people thought of it only to suspect it, and preferred General Jackson to all the statesmen the Bank could muster to its standards." From the Lehrman Institute of American history.

Here again we need to connect the dots of history to find what Wilson was trying to say. He says. After the people showed support for Jackson. The banks couldn't compete in popularity with the President. In Wilson's opinion, it was much easier for the common men to believe Jackson when he said the banks are dangerous and corrupted. (*Jackson perhaps another ordinary person in Wilson's view*). Than for the common man to understand the arguments of statesmen. This your basic put down to from a snob to ordinary people. In this case, people like Wilson speaking in regards of the services provided by the banks to the government and to commerce. In other words, the common men, was incapable to grasp the lofty words of political leaders like Wilson of course. The banking business is way too unfair to the consumer Wilson knew that. I wonder if he ever hear or considered the word "Equitable" It just does not exist in Wilson's vocabulary. Do you know why the bankers can make hundreds of times more money than their depositors? It's thanks to that deceiving practice called "Fractional Deposit". Where they can lend nine times more money that they do not have. This an immoral racket is the scam they work with. What gives them the right? It's absurd and irrational. How many times do they have prove us they are after is dishonest profit. So, here we go again. In the eyes of Wilson, we would try the same scheme one more time expecting different results. Isn't this how we define insanity? Wilson had to immerse his head deep in Zionist garbage to think that his assessment was superior to Jackson. Rather than seeking flattery from the elite. President Jackson fought and risk his life to preserve the blessing of liberty for all Americans. Wilson instead, gave it away to the bankers in a silver platter. Jackson went through great lengths to show the vicious ambitions Biddle and the bankers had in-store for the American people. The Americans of the Jackson era acted as if we are not buying Biddle's crap. This made them more shrewd and aware than being incapable. Something that Wilson preferred to think. Wilson was wrong in writing that Jackson disliked the banks only on instinct. This where I think Wilson was trying to deceive us. You see. Rather than dislike the bankers on intuition Jackson educated himself. He told the bankers I have read the South Sea Bubble gentlemen. The scam perpetrated by the banks in England in 1712. Because this event, Jackson thought, that was enough reason to suspect the scamming bankers. But like a good Zionist bureaucrat that wasn't enough for Wilson. Can you tell who played the pawn and who was strong for America Jackson did a great job of telling his suspicion of the banks into the public who supported him. Of course for Wilson this was an aberration, and insult that in his view needed correction. How dare them to support Jackson and not the demagogue Biddle and the upper class. Wilson, another demagogue, once he thought he had a shoot at the White House he saw the opportunity to impose his changes to the country with total discount for the will of the people.

He was faithful to work for the Zionist elite and he did his job in spades. He knew the legislation senator Nelson Aldrich presented in Congress was the works of Zionist bankers of New York. But the supreme mastermind behind the scenes was Baron Alfred Rothschild of London. Their public campaign for Wilson was a masterful piece. As I said before. These people are scientists. They went ahead and gave interviews condemning the bill that they have created and promoted. This is what you call reverse psychology. They caused people to believe if bankers think that this is a bad bill for them it must be good for us. Scholars of the most prominent universities went on writing beautiful essays for the banker's bill If you don't think this is possible. Stop and think for a moment. Remember Secretary of State Colin Powell (CFR) at the UN. His brilliant dissertation to prove Iraq's possession of weapons of mass destruction? We believed him and the information he gave us. As a result, we went on to support the inept President George W. Busch. However, the result of this deception caused us to go to war with Iraq. Now, Saddam Hussein was no saint of my devotion, but the bank of Iraq was not under the Federal Reserve's control. Rumor has it Saddam Hussein for several years had veered away from selling Iraq's oil in US dollars, but Euros as his currency of choice. He made significant earning when the US dollar lost more than 20% to the Euro. Well, after more than five thousand American lives lost and more than a million Iraqis dead this Zionist war was won. Iraq sells its oil in US dollars again, and the bank of Iraq is now under the Federal Reserve clutch. I think that should tell us something; or maybe it's only a coincidence, nothing to worry about.

Let us take another piece of evidence to learn more about Nicholas Biddle and our good old President Wilson. Let it be no doubt that Wilson was much in bed with the Zionist, he was happy to sign the Federal Reserve into law, and never expressed any reason for remorse. Wilson know well the history behind Biddle. He knew what Biddle did when he engaged in a political and economic duel with President Jackson. This comes from the Lerhman Institute of American history.

In early March 1834. Biddle wrote that Jackson. "By removing the public revenues has relieved the Bank from all responsibility for the currency". The historians Wright and Cowen wrote. "Biddle should have responded as he had in 1825, adding liquidity to the system to calm investors' nerves. But he stopped acting as the nation's central bank, seeking only to save himself and his institution. Instead of extending credit, Biddle curtained it drastically. He did this hoping to induce a recession that would force Americans, and Jackson, to beg for mercy.

There cannot be no doubt of Biddle's purposes. It's clear that Biddle had no qualms in putting the screws to the American people. Or anybody (including the President) who dared not to do business with Mr. Central Bank Biddle. If you remove your deposits I can go ahead and devaluate the currency and your buying power, be gone. Biddle is giving us a clear example that he can turn on a dime and do an about-face to save his own hide and his beloved central bank. Meanwhile, his actions would cause a recession on the working class of America. But like an expert slave master. Only to chock them, but not to kill them; any good slave master wants to preserve his slaves, after all they are the prime source of profits. I think here Biddle shows us his true colors such arrogance, and ego, makes him an egocentric. Further, Biddle the villain expected us to trust him. He wanted to be in-charge of our currency, without any supervision, and answerable to no one. Sounds like Alan Greenspan doesn't it.

I mean, was Biddle something or what!

This is a true picture of Nicholas Biddle. This is what you expect from a Central Bank manager and Wilson knew it. Biddle single-handed caused a recession because President Jackson dared to defy him. We should ask Wilson as we can ask Obama. What is the sense of having a government of the people and for the people if thugs like Biddle or Yellen are in control? The most important aspect of being free is in the government's ability to control the money supply. If by disgrace this falls on people like Biddle, who couldn't give a rat's ass about you or the country. Well guys it's time to grab your ankles because we are doomed. They betrayal of Woodrow Wilson is so huge we have no law to fit his crime. However, it doesn't mean we cannot pass judgment. Where does the American Revolution stand if an American president was willing to surrender it to the slave drivers Zionist bankers? History should have judged Wilson and his cronies for subversion, conspiracy, and treason. They caused to overthrow a free government by controlling the money resulting in the control of the branches of government that guarantee its autonomy. Having friends like Woodrow Wilson who needs enemies. Sadly, today we have many Woodrow Wilsons in our mist working for the Zionist. They have infiltrated all branches of government, the top private sectors and in every part of human strive.

A private monopoly of money would be inherently dangerous to the nation. President Jackson once said. Back in Jackson's days the Central Bank had twenty-five directors. The government picked five. The other twenty directors the Central Bank picked them. Because this grotesque disparity the bank's majority overrun the interest of the public. Today we don't even have that. Today we don't even get to choose one director. Because its influence the Federal Reserve selects our next Secretary of the Treasury. Remember Timothy Geithner?

We cannot grasp the idea someone has the power to create money out of nothing. It's hard to think how you would feel having that much power. But the Zionist have tasted this power and like sweet evil poison they like it. Rest assured they would do anything to keep that power. It's like having the memorable Goose that lays the Golden Eggs in your hands. I guess here will be a good time to bring this quote from Mayer Amschel Rothschild.

"Let me issue and control a nation's money and I care not who writes the laws."

In 1863 in a letter written to their associates in New York these Rothschild explains how our present banking industry works:

"The few who understand the system, will either be so interested in its profits or be so dependent upon its favors, that there will be no opposition from that class, while on the other hand, the great body of people, mentally incapable of comprehending the tremendous advantage that capital derives from the system, will bear its burdens without complaint, and perhaps without even suspecting that the system is inimical to their interests."

The Rothschild brothers of London writing to associates in New York, 1863

These people know we are gullible, and so easy to fleece. Believing these power hungry Rothschild is like believing the promise of a white shark that it's not going to bite you. I remember this wise old saying. "In an opened chest even the righteous sin". These men are far from righteous and they have control over the awesome power of the nation's money? Many times over these men have proved they don't have a shred of decency. Or morality, fairness, or honesty in their veins. Would you put a pack of wolves in charge of the sheep heard? Well, that is exactly what Woodrow Wilson did when he signed the Federal Reserve into law. It doesn't take a genius to figure out these packs of Zionist wolves. With the money supply in their control they are free to carry out any evil plan in their agenda. Feeling omnipotent and answerable to no one like Allen Greenspan said it. The Zionist bankers have made great strides throughout the twentieth century. They continue today into the Twenty-first century with hardly any opposition. Why? Because they keep us ignorant. They control the news media, the education, the military and religion, you may think they have won and we have no hope, but we do. You see, all we need is to wake up 3% of the population. The United States population is about 330 million 3% out of that is about ten million. If we take 10% out of the 10 million we have one million and with one million we march to Washington. Believe me one million people in front of Congress will persuade to abolish the Federal Reserve. The quicker people learn these facts, the worse it is for the Federal Reserve.

It was the Attorney General Roger B. Taney, who saw right through Biddle's recharter bill. He looked at it as a form of political blackmail. In his words:

"Now, as I understand the application at the present time, it means if the Bank says to the President, your next election is at hand - if you charter us, well - if not, beware."

The historian H.W. Brands tells us that Roger Taney presented evidence to President Jackson. Evidence that Biddle had manipulated the money supply before the last congressional session. Biddle motivation was to act by what he thought best for his beloved bank. Taney went as far on to show that Biddle had bought favorable press coverage for the bank during the fight for renewal of the charter. This practice of employing the people's money to manipulate the democratic process was pregnant with so much evil. Taney told Jackson, that it alone was cause for the severest censure.

If we understand that in the past the bankers needed to use the press for their evil purposes. Today it's much easier. Since the

Federal Reserve and perhaps a few years before, the Zionist bankers started to buy out all the most important newspapers in America. After that, came radio, movie studios, television, cable news, magazines, you name it. It's under control. This is how today, these Zionists don't have any problem moving their plans forward. With the aid of Zionists journalists like Wolf Blitzer of CNN and others like him. They contribute and control the printed page and so the thinking of today.

The Zionist have programmed and designed your circle of understanding. It's difficult for the average citizen trying to get a grip of these cumbersome ideas. Getting a grip of the Zionists agenda can be awkward, painful and frustrating. Especially if have been a sleep all your life trying to get your head out of the sand for the first time is also painful and frustrating. When you remove your blinders to see the reality of the world can be awaking and a beautiful experience. Remember the movie "The Matrix". It remains me the dramatic moment when Neo woke up from the Matrix. Neo sees the world for the first time. Neo is awake no longer sees the fantasy world he believed since childhood. He asked. "Why my eyes hurt" Morpheus answered. "Because Neo you have never used them before". Consider yourself at the first stage of a long journey my dear reader. You have chosen the red pill and you're waking up!

The evidence speaks volumes loud and clear. For all the advances the Zionists have made in the last one hundred years, we must begin to admit the United States of America is no longer a democracy, or a republic. It's a corporation in the hands of the Zionists bankers. Since December 23, 1913 a day like December 7, 1941 should live in infamy. We have lived with the illusion that freedom and democracy are part of our way of life, but that's long gone now. Since 9/11 and the Patriot Act our freedoms have been reduced drastically. They say it's necessary for our national security and to fight terrorism, but you know it's all an invention. The powerful Zionist can create events and carry out to make prophesies become realities. Contrary to biblical prophesy this is the case of the unbiblical creation of the Zionist state of Israel in 1947. The biblical scholar Theodore Pike explains to us with these words:

"In regards to the Jews, I consider it's the duty of every man and woman to open their eyes about the Zionist Jews. But it's not our duty to assure them that a land of promise, may be occupied without obedience. Neither is it our duty to fight a war in the Middle East in defense of Israel's unbiblical claim."

The key we need to understand here is obedience to God. The problem is that whatever God the Jews obey today is a total perversion. The UN is of Zionist Origen and serves the Zionist agenda more often than you care to count. Leave it to the Rothschild family money and influence to cause Israel to become a reality. Today it's estimated that more than 80% of the land in Israel are on Rothschild property. But perhaps it's only coincidence, nothing to worry about.

The slavery that Woodrow Wilson signed us in is what I call the equal opportunity slavery. In today's slavery there is no distinction of race, sex, creed, or religion; everybody is part of the herd. Leo Tolstoy the famous Russian novelist and philosopher, author of the famous novel War and Peace puts it this way:

"Money is a new form of slavery, and distinguishable from the old simply by the fact that it is impersonal – that there is no human relation between master and slave." Leo Tolstoy.

What I find most extraordinary and mindboggling is this quote inaccurately credited to Sir Josiah Stamp. He was president of the Bank of England in 1928, and the second richest man in Britain.

"Banking was conceived in iniquity and was born in sin. The bankers own the earth. Take it away from them, but leave them the power to create money, and with the flick of the pen they will create

enough deposits to buy it back again. However, take away from them the power to create money and all the great fortunes like mine will disappear and they ought to disappear, for this would be a happier and better world to live in. But, if you wish to remain the slaves of bankers and pay the cost of your own slavery, let them continue to create money".

Usually at the highest levels of banking you will not find a repented banker. It will be like finding a vegetarian white shark. It just doesn't happen. As an international banker he have received training in the arts of deceiving. It's part of his being and training like an Army officer. He is to receive the program, and indoctrination necessary to carry out his job as efficient and gainfully as possible. That's a Zionist banker. I wanted to insert Josiah Stamp asserted quote anyway because I think that is so accurate and true in it's content. Still, I want to bring you another example from another prominent banker. His quote is coming straight from his memoirs, his name is David Rockefeller. David puts it this way.

"For more than a century ideological extremist at either end of the political spectrum have seized upon well-publicized incidents...such as my encounter with Castro to attack the Rockefeller family for the inordinate influence they claim we wield over American political and economical institutions. Some even believe we are part of a secret cabal working against the best interest of the United States, characterizing my family and me as internationalist...and of conspiring with others around the world to build a more integrated global political and economic structure; one world, if you will. If that is the charge, I stand guilty, and I am proud of it." David Rockefeller Memoirs 2002 pg 405

David Rockefeller is a well-known Zionist. He is co-owner of the Federal Reserve and the founder of the infamous Trilateral Commission. He owns Chase Bank and many well-known insurance companies, oil companies and more. His fortune is well into the trillions of dollars. David is that Zionist that by his words he couldn't be more clear. He's omnipotent, he has so much power under his command that he has no qualms admitting it. He's an internationalist. He willingly works against the best interest of the United States, his country of birth. So, he admits he is seditious and provably betrays his country every day. But he couldn't care less. If you know he's part of a secret global cabal working to achieve the NOW (New World Order) in other words, the Zionist agenda. David Rockefeller is the result of the scam the Federal Reserve have run for the last one hundred year in this country. David Rockefeller admits it in his memoirs. Still, if we could take away his power to make money out of nothing,. We wouldn't have the Rockefeller or Rothschild to worry about. Creeps like these just couldn't become so powerful. Let us take a look at some of the results that Woodrow Wilson greatest achievement left us with.

Chapter 4

Results of the Creation of the Federal Reserve

To understand the results of creating the Federal Reserve we need to learn what were the reasons to create it first. Then, discover how the Zionist bankers could achieve such a monumental goal. As I mentioned before in 1907 JP Morgan set into motion a calculated banking crisis. Let's not forget that JP Morgan was a Rothschild agent. He was already working under the orders of the Rothschild of London. Thus, it's safe to say that this little crisis was a Rothschild maneuver. On mid-October 1907 JP Morgan started a rumor the Knickerbocker Bank was insolvent. As a result of this rumor JP Morgan caused such a fear in the people they run to the bank to get their money. (This was like shouting fire in a movie theater). This created crisis caused the bank to call its pending loans, thus, before you know it you had a panic and a crisis in your hands. This crisis by JP Morgan design caused the stock market to lose almost 50% of its value in less than a month. That was JP Morgan at his best ladies and gentleman. What marks this deed of shame for JP Morgan immoral, and total depravity. Is that JP Morgan himself offered the solution by printing money out of his bank. To help quail the crisis that he helped to create. JP Morgan in a most shameless act started to make money out of nothing, and to add salt to an open wound. Surprise! Congress let him do it! So, with the blessing of Congress Morgan made $300,000,000 dollars of this rubbish private money. Because there was no one to stop him. He used it to buy plummeting stocks of healthy corporations for pennies to the dollar. He even sent some of this funny money to his branch banks to lend at interest! JP Morgan the fraud and a con artist was hailed as a hero by the then President of Princeton University, Woodrow Wilson. He was so deeply touched by this selfless act that he declared:

"All this trouble could be averted if we appointed a committee of six or seven public spirited men like J. P. Morgan, to handle the affairs of our country."

What a schmuck!

Everything worked out perfect for the pirate Morgan. As a result, the crisis of 1907 helped him to solidify a prefer position as a Rothschild agent in America. This little crisis was of course was just a warm up, just the beginning. JP Morgan and his Zionist cronies were preparing us up for what was real deal the main event, to create the Federal Reserve. JP Morgan helped to secure a windfall of profits and assets for the Rothschild. Even more important JP Morgan helped to create the right set of circumstances for the people in America to become more susceptible to change. People begun to believe that a central bank was not such a bad idea as long it can prevent another panic like the one they just went through. The plotting never stop and the ruling elite went to work.

Because of this financial crisis in 1908 President Theodore Roosevelt signed into law to create the National Monetary Commission. Senator Nelson Aldrich (R) from Connecticut was the chairperson. What we never learned and we need to know is this commission was under siege from the beginning by JP Morgan pals and cronies. Just like the 9/11 commission comprised of George W. Busch pals and cronies. Nelson Aldrich was notorious for his close business relations with the big banks of New York. Yet, they went on to Europe wasting $300,000 of taxpayer's money for a two year tour on a fact finding mission to report to Congress. They went on to study the intricacies of the central banks of England, France and Germany, but wait a minute! Weren't all these banks under Rothschild control already! So, if we connect the dots here this commission didn't go to study banking European style. They went to learn the Rothschild way of doing dirty banking. Okay... I get it! What a slap in the face of the American people.

How would this sleazy bankers pull this off? Because by 1910 after Aldrich and his commission returned from Europe with a bunch of books. Made many politicians in Congress expressed misgivings about a central bank. They were suspicious of that vault of books Senator Aldrich brought back from Europe. They knew of his close business ties to JP Morgan. Besides, Aldrich had ties to the Rockefellers by his daughter's marriage to John D. Rockefeller. For that matter Nelson Aldrich first try to present this legislation got thumbs-down in Congress. He couldn't possibly sell it but he wasn't going to give up. So, he changed the bill around a little bit and picked two democrats to present the bill. Senator, Robert L. Owen of Oklahoma, and Representative Carter Glass of Virginia. What became the Owen-Glass Federal Reserve Act. With all these state of affairs in Aldrich's favor the stage for the coup moved forward. It was a merciless political battle you had the Zionist bankers focused and committed to creating the Federal Reserve, and Congress rightfully so rejecting the idea. We should expect with some serious opposition in Congress the Zionist were going to use every trick and whatever means of deception available to achieve this goal. That's exactly what they did. The Federal Reserve is the result of a shameful cartel of white-collar crooks. Far from an organization of respectable, honorable men dedicated to service the American people.

It was autumn in 1910 and Senator Nelson Aldrich back in America called on Abraham Piatt Andrew. He was a commission member and assistant professor of economics at Harvard University. Aldrich asked him to start drafting in secret the remedial legislation using the books they brought back from Europe. For Nelson Aldrich and his cronies time were of the essence. They have to move fast. So, on the night of November 22, 1910, in the railway station at

Hoboken, New Jersey the legion of doom was about to leave. They planned a deceptive duck hunting trip southbound to Jekyll Island off the coast of Georgia. The public record today allows us to mention all these men by name. They have earned their place the shameful hall of fame as the founders and architects of the Federal Reserve. Like a gang of white-collar thugs they were about to commit the biggest coup d'etat ever perpetrated on any nation in the world. So, here we begin their names. First is Senator Nelson Aldrich. He was the Republican whip in the Senate and chairperson of the National Monetary Commission. Nelson Aldrich supposedly worked on legislation to break the grip of the big banks in New York, instead he did exactly the opposite, he sided with them. Second, Abraham Piatt Andrew, by now he became assistant secretary of the Treasury. This guy was like a double agent, he was a federal employee and knowing well what he was doing went to work for the bankers. Farm boy, Frank Vanderlip. He was an expert in commercial banking, and President of National City Bank of New York, the biggest bank in America. Henry Davison was the Senior Partner of the JP Morgan Company, also an expert in investing banking. Another heavy player was Mr. Charles Norton the president of the First National bank of New York. Also Benjamin Strong he was the head of the JP Morgan Bankers Trust Company. Mr. Strong was a friend of Woodrow Wilson that after the Federal Reserve passed, he became its first chairperson. I saved for last Mr. Paul Warburg, the only German born, naturalized American citizen, partner in Kuhn Loeb & Co. Paul was representative agent of the Rothschild in England and France. His brother Max Warburg was managing partner at M.M. Warburg, one of the largest private equity banks in Germany. Together Max with his brother Felix Warburg helped finance Germany during WWI. It was Kaiser Wilhelm, who chose Max Warburg as head of Germany's secret service during WWI. And while they were busy financing Germany, our good old brother Paul Warburg of Kuhn Loeb & Co. was financing the American side.

To improve and display how close the bankers of England and Germany worked with their American associates I offer this anecdote that occurred in 1915. The British nurse Edith Cavell worked in a teaching hospital in Belgium, she was shot by a German firing squad on October 12, 1915. Her crime was to report to London the Allied "Belgian Relief Commission" (charged with feeding Belgium) was in fact sending thousands of tons of supplies to Germany. Edith's act of bravery caused Sir William Wiseman, the head of British Intelligence, and partner in the bankers Kuhn, Loeb, to demand from the Germans to execute Cavell as a spy. The Germans reluctantly complied, but was possible because Wiseman knew Paul Warburg very well from Kuhn, Loeb and Paul's brother Max was chief of German Intelligence. This despicable conspiracy between the bankers from Germany, England and the United States made them worry because it could shorten the duration of the war and thus, reduce profits for both sides.

The Rothschild and the Warburg have had control of the bank of Germany for a long time. Now WWI would bring them closer to world domination with the creation of the League of Nations. One of their main goals and for that they went to work over-time printing debt money to finance both sides. It is of particular importance to point out that all this was happening right under the nose of our Nobel Peace Prize winner our beloved president Woodrow Wilson.

You would think that this information is taught to our students in high school or college; nothing further from the truth. The official version of the creation of the FED is explained to our students by the celebrated economist Paul A. Samuelson. In his book, first published in 1948 "Economics: An Introductory Analysis" became the immediate authority for the principles of economics courses until today, and he says.

"It (the Federal Reserve) sprang from the panic of 1907 with its alarming epidemic of bank failures: the country was fed up once and for all with the anarchy of unstable private banking."

From Paul A. Samuelson book titled "Economics".

Paul Samuelson was an American with a PhD in economics from Harvard; his book was the best seller of all-time. He won a Nobel Memorial Prize in Economic Sciences. The Swiss Academy considered he raised the level of scientific analysis in economic theory more than any other present-day economist. Samuelson has earned the title "Father of Modern Economics". The New York Times named him "leading academic economist of the 20th century". President Bill Clinton. He praised Samuelson for his "fundamental contributions to economic science" for over 60 years. Impressive, don't you think? I just wish he would have raised the level of awareness in the American people. He could have denounced the few dominant, merciless and vicious Zionist men in charge of our economy. Samuelson had the power to disclose how vicious and immoral is the control of the nation's money in Zionist hands. Let's keep in mind that is the Zionist do a great job to manipulate history, education and so the ideas of a brilliant man like Samuelson. According to Samuelson and the Jekyll Island Legion of Doom the most important reason of creating the Federal Reserve was to come up with a lender-of-last-resort in moments of imminent crisis. To keep the economy stable, firm, secured, steadfast, permanent and enduring. This is the lie JP Morgan and associates sold the public after the made up panic of 1907.

Here we introduce William F. Donnelly and his book "American Economic Growth": The Historic Challenge. Donnelly states the Jekyll Islanders; as he calls them. Sought to correct the most obvious defects in American banking. That is the inflexibility of the bond-secured currency. And the immobility of bank reserves, with as little dislocation of banking practices as possible. In other words, they wanted to create flexible currency, meaning fiat money, money created out of thin air. Thus, charge interest on it, just like JP Morgan did in 1907 but this time they wanted to make it official. The immobility of bank reserves you translate to the fraudulent fractional deposits. This insidious practice gives banks the ability to lend nine times more money than they have.

To explain. If you make a deposit for $1000.00 dollars, the bank can take this $1000.00 make it a 10% reserve and lend $9000.00 at interest. While they pay you less than 1% for your deposit they can make say a conservative 4%. Multiply than 9 times and you have 36% interest that belongs to the bank. This is the scam they wanted to make legal by passing the Federal Reserve Act. According to Donnelly, the Jekyll Islanders wanted to take the government out of the banking business. According to Jekyll Islanders the government should stay out. I don't suppose they ever read the Constitution. And if they ever read it, they couldn't care less. Ruthless and deceitful as they are. These Zionists bankers moved against the Constitution. After all this was a Rothschild coup d'état and the Rothschild philosophy is:

"Let me issue and control a nation's money and I care not who writes the laws".

That's the bottom line, isn't it; control and power.

On Jekyll Island the Legion of Doom went to work immediately and with intensity. I must point out these bankers before they gather in Jekyll Island were competitors. However, if they wanted to create the Federal Reserve, they would need to put aside their mistrust and work together for their common goal. Under the Rothschild flag this competitors, came together to form a banking cartel called the monopoly of money. After nine days of hammering out it was Paul Warburg who came with the name Federal. Let's call it Federal so people would think this is another Federal agency. Next, let's call it Reserve, that you might think there is something in reserve. Last, let's call it a system. They needed to add the word system to complete this deception. This fake system of banks would deceive the public into believing the Money Trust would finally lose its grip. The idea of system carried more weight than it does today. They created twelve banks in different locations. But it was the New York Branch the most powerful and important. This is the deception, the ploy, the swindle President Wilson and his Money Trust cronies pulled on all of us. Conversely, had Congress or the public cut wind of this meeting at Jekyll Island Congress would have shut down the legislation. That's why absolute secrecy was essential for them to succeed! For many years they all denied this meeting ever took place. It was on February 9, 1935, the Saturday Evening Post printed an article written by the eyewitness Frank Vanderlip. This is a little piece of his autobiography, his grandson was kind to provide. Here, Frank spills the beans:

"I do not feel it is any exaggeration to speak of our secret expedition to Jekyll Island as the occasion of the actual conception of what eventually became the Federal Reserve System. We were told to leave our last names behind us. We were told further that we should avoid dining together on the night of our departure. We were instructed to come one at a time and as unobtrusively as possible to the railroad terminal on the New Jersey littoral of the Hudson where Senator Aldrich's private car would be in readiness attached to the rear-end of a train to the south. Once aboard the private car we began to observe the taboo that had been fixed on last names. We addressed one another as Ben, Paul, Nelson and Abe. Davison and I adopted even deeper disguises abandoning our first names. On the theory that we were always right, he became Wilbur and I became Orville after those two aviation pioneers the Wright brothers. The servants and train crew may have known the identities of one or two of us, but they did not know all and it was the names of all printed together that would've made our mysterious journey significant in Washington, in Wall Street, even in London. Discovery we knew simply must not happen. If it were to be

exposed publicly that our particular group had gotten together and written a banking bill, that bill would have no chance whatever of passage by Congress." Yet, who was there in Congress who might have drafted a sound piece of legislation dealing with the purely banking problem with which we were concerned?"

Vanderlip knew of politicians in Congress opposing the idea of a central bank. But more important, he believed there was no one qualified to produce such legislation. Assuming this was true, Vanderlip who had knowledge in American and banking history must have known about Nicolas Trist private secretary of President Andrew Jackson. When reflecting on the awesome power the privately owned Second Bank of the United States had; Trist said.

"The bare existence of such a power is a thing irreconcilable with the nature and spirit of our institutions." (Schlesinger, The Age of Jackson, p.102)

"Irreconcilable with the nature and spirit of our institutions, and our Constitution." This is the quote every true and descent American must whole dear if we pledge alliance to the flag and have sworn to defend our Constitution against enemies foreign and domestic. Vanderlip, who had full knowledge that the banking business nature is deception and mistrust. If he had a shred of decency should have been a little bit more honest; look around his peers in Jekyll Island and say: "We are not qualified"

Sadly and disappointing the self-centered Legion of Doom believed divine and infallible have the duty to rule over the rest of the world. So, with this attitude in mind they exerted their self-appointed right to control the currency of this nation and the world as it's their self-appointed right. These delusional people are fully aware what they can do with this awesome power. Once they control the money, they have the capacity to control governments, politicians, education, the military, and religion. In essence, with no question everything, and unchallenged. A corporation working like the Federal

Reserve represents everything America does not stand for. Every day the Federal Reserve is at work brings one more day of shame to us. You must ask yourself. Who's job is more important? The Zionist collaborators helping perpetrate the lie? Or the fearless few trying to open your eyes. If what the Federal Reserve does to the world doesn't qualify as world domination or New World Order then, what qualifies. This is the reality Zionist domination has brought to America. We will arm ourselves with equal strength, and we are going to start fighting back. One by one we are going to start throwing a monkey wrench in their plans until they realize they can no longer get their way. They will soon know the American people is a force they have to reckon with. Together we are stronger, and we would be invisible. We would become vigilant like a hawk watching and fighting back.

The bankers knew to make their bill pass they were going to meet strong resistance in Congress. Especially by a few senators who could show integrity. Senators like Charles Lindbergh had the courage the expose this fraud with these words:

"From now on, depressions will be scientifically created. This Federal Reserve Act establishes the most gigantic trust on earth. When the President (Wilson) signs this bill, the invisible government of the monetary power will be legalized....the worst legislative crime of the ages is perpetrated by this banking and currency bill." -- Charles A. Lindbergh, Sr. 1913.

The greatest example of depression was in 1929. This depression brought famine to America. And recently, the Zionist Ben Shalom Bernanke, the former Federal Reserve chairman admitted the Federal Reserve caused the Great Depression. One interesting fact Bernanke omitted to this admission. The crash in 1929 all the members of the Money Trust miraculously pulled out.

But it's only a coincidence, nothing to worry about!

Our most recent example is of course the 2008 crisis. This financial debacle could've been easy to avoid if someone would have listened to Brooksley Born. She was the former head of the Commodity Futures Trading Commission (CFTC). Born went on to try to disclose the dangers of derivatives. She noticed this (WMD) Weapons of Mass Deception traded without much controls. And Born became alarmed by the lack of government oversight. Derivatives were a secretive, multitrillion-dollar over-the-counter market. When she continued to ask questions and tried to regulate them, she woke up to a most unpleasant surprise. She had to confront with the fierce resistance from then-Fed Chairman Alan Greenspan. The Treasury Secretary Robert Rubin, and Deputy Treasury Secretary Larry Summers respectively. All these hard core Zionists prevailed on Congress to stop Born and limit future regulations. After Born proposed to regulate Derivatives Greenspan, Rubin and the former SEC head Arthur Levitt made this extraordinary statement. For them Congress should pass legislation that prevents CFTC from oversight. If this is not prepotent attitude I don't know what is. To think they can suede the Congress of the United States to legislate in their favor. To continue committing abuses and crimes against our economy is appalling and inexcusable. This should tell us the Zionist work their own political agenda. The fact these jackals call themselves Jews without a drop of Semite blood is one thing. But you don't need to be a Jew to be Zionist as the VP Joe Biden clearly said it to Israeli TV.

Do you think these Zionist have anything to do with running the country? I mean if they can prevent the head of a Federal agency from doing her job? If they can muster enough political clout in Congress to get what they want. You have to give it to them, they have gained and secure enough positions of power that enable them to advance their agenda effectively. The Rabbi Ovadia Yosef explained why exist the Zionist craving to insatiable greed and conquest. He went on record in the Jerusalem Post. The most important newspaper in the Zionist State of Israel.

"Gentiles exist only to serve Jews. The Goyim was born only to serve us. They have no place in the world other than to serve the people of Israel. He goes on to answer why are gentiles needed:"Why are gentiles needed? They will work, they will plow, they will sow, and they will reap. We will sit like an Effendi (Master) and eat. That is why gentiles were created."

This is exactly the theory that drives the Zionist bankers of Wall Street and the Federal Reserve. They represent the greatest a menace to us and the world. They are in true the greatest foe America has yet to face. A great book that explains this further is "Crisis by Design" written by John Truman Wolfe. He is the former chairperson of the Department of History at John F. Kennedy University. Also, former senior credit officer for banks in San Francisco and Beverly Hills. This book has great insights to help you understand the Zionist agenda. Let's go back now to the Federal Reserve and examine whether they've delivered on the promise to keep the economy stable. Let us examine if those promises were their true objectives. Shall we?

Since 1913 the Federal Reserve it has presided over the stock crash of 1921. The stock market crash of 1929. The great depression of 1929 to 1939 where they decrease the money supply rather than increase it making matters worse. Recessions in the years: 1953, 1957, 1969, 1975, 1981. The stock market crash in 1987, "Black Monday". And the latest and the greatest villainy of the Wall Street boys the 2008 Crisis. This debacle is still lingering, despite the optimist pundits we still have a long way to recover. You can call me irresponsible. But, not even the best football coach keeps his job after so many failures. So why the Federal Reserve keeps its job after one hundred years of boom and bust economy? It has failed miserably, deserves the boot and put out of business! The justification is simple. Most Americans still believed the Federal Reserve is just another Federal agency. Thus, like any bureaucracy, we think we cannot get rid of it. Sure, we can! And we must send them to oblivion! The Federal Reserve is no more federal than Federal Express. And the more people learn of its fraudulent practices the quicker they are going to face their downfall. I would argue. The downfall of the Federal Reserve would be far more significant than fall the Berlin Wall, or fall the Soviet Union. Collapsing the Federal Reserve would mean liberty not only for America but for the whole world too.

The Money Trust never showed concern with keeping a stable economy. First, They concerned that fewer people went to the banks asking for a loan. Because banks consider this is the core of their business they wanted to stop this eroding power trend. Why? In those days the working class of America had buying power. People and businesses could save for their projects; this is what we call private capital formation. Second, they need to reverse this trend by enticing the people to come and borrow money. How do you do that? Remember they said the nation needed a flexible currency. The problem is this flexible currency is money they create out of nothing. And they charge you interest on it when you borrow. The Federal Reserve gave them this capacity. This is why you see Bernanke lowering interest rates to 0.25%. Why do you think he can afford that? Because if you charge interest out of something that cost you nothing to create; you still can show a profit. Don't you? Interest rates are in the hands of the Federal Reserve something did not exist before 1913. I once heard Bernanke saying. If necessary, he would bring up or down the interest rate within fifteen minutes. Here is something our legislators, free press news media should think about. We are a society proud in having freedom of enterprise. Then, If we want freedom of enterprise not the Federal Reserve or corporation should have control of the interest rates. It should fall and rise because the natural forces of supply and demand to decide interest rates. The third objective was to pass the losses to the taxpayer for people's sake. We have eye witnessed this villainy, this treachery in 2008. You saw Henry Paulson the secretary of Treasury, and Goldmanite at heart handy work. He gathered Congress and in record time pulled together 700 billion dollar bailout money the TARP money. This money intended for the big banks responsible for the crisis to begin with. Why do we have to pay for the banker's failures? Because their failure could trigger another Great Depression. These banks have declared they cannot go down they are too big to fail. Says who! The Goldmanites! And because they control the show. That much we know. This is a direct outcome of signing the Federal Reserve into law giving control of the currency to the Zionist Bankers. This how you can see that we surrendered our sovereignty the day Woodrow Wilson signed the Federal Reserve into law. Today the powerful Money Trust is 30% bigger than in 2008. They have gained even more control of the world economy and world events. They work as a dictatorship, democracy is nothing but an illusion.

If you have any doubt how the Zionist infestation run Congress remember senator Chuck Hagel. How he collapsed, buckled, and recanted in front of the Senate Armed Services Committee. The Zionist shills presented devastating audio clips to convince the world Hagel is Anti-Israel. The funny thing is that they all knew about it a long time ago. Thus, no one in his right mind should have suggested Chuck Hagel for Secretary of Defense. With these clips Hagel's nomination was problematic at best. On the day of his dissertation in front of his fellow senators Hagel might have felt he was in a viper's nest. Senators Ted Cruz, Roger Wicker and Lindsey Graham all Zionist shills went to work. They decided to thank him for his services, give him a bloody nose, mop the floor with his ass and then give him the nomination. What a humiliation to a decorated Vietnam vet. This is how the Senate hearing went for Chuck. Senator Cruz asked Hagel if Israel has committed war crimes Hagel recanted, and said no, when he should have said yes! I said it before Senator Cruz and I say it again now; and here I make my case. Instead Hagel looked frail, feeble, puny, and pathetic. Hagel continued taking more crap when Senator Graham asked him to name one senator influenced by the Jewish Lobby. He said "I don't know" When his answer should have been: you and I senator to begin with. Why is my nomination for US Secretary of Defense depending on whether I would defend Israel? If Zionist influence was nonexistent we wouldn't be having this conversation now, would we? But, no one defended the secretary of defense. The Zionist wanted Hagel to learn his lesson. Hagel learned who his real boss is before he got the nomination. Isn't that humiliating? America, the land of the Free and home of the Brave we decide our Secretary of Defense under the influence of Zionist Israel. We must consider this calamity is result of the Zionist influence at the highest levels of government.

Most politicians are like diapers; we need to change them often and for the same reason. The Zionist shills that beat-up on Hagel; are the politicians we need to vote out. For every rule has an exception and for us poor souls that exception means hope and that hope is Senator Elizabeth Warren. She is new to the senate, but she understands what the Giga bankers of New York are all about. She started by creating the Consumer Protection Bureau. Against all odds and little hope for the middle and low income class in America. Still, the Consumer Protection Bureau is now a reality. The CPB is protecting consumers against predatory lending and outrageous credit card interest rates. Without this protection young servicemen and women in the Naval Air Station NAS Norfolk, Virginia would receive 600% to 700% interest for a loan. The lender is Norfolk gave a new definition for a loan shark. With this protection the same service member could receive not higher than 36% interest. Still too high for service members we put in harm's way yet, better than 700%. As a result, Senator Warren has been already under the Zionist Giga Bankers eyes as a problem they have to deal with. For her sake, I can only hope and pray that she can take precautions. Senator Warren is presumably a candidate to the presidency. They are comparing her with Hillary Clinton, perhaps for her dynamism, but I say, you there is nothing else to compare. While Senator Elizabeth Warren wears and armor of honesty and integrity. Hillary wears an armor made of lies and deceit. Let me recommend a great documentary made to certify, to bear out, what a fraud Hillary Clinton is and why she needs to put out to pasture and close the book on her. Watch "Hillary Clinton Exposed". This film is directed by Alan Peterson. He is an accomplished movie director. And written by Michael Wright a screenwriter professor at the University of Tulsa, Oklahoma. This film is a must see for those blind followers who still consider Hillary to run for president in 2016. Just one clip worth mentioning in this film is Hillary's M.O. for P.R. or her Modus Operandi for Public Relations. What she means to say is. "Say what you need to say at any given moment. And rely on the lack of memory of the American people and the support of mainstream media to support that lack of memory". This is precisely what the Zionist Bankers of New York have used over the past one hundred years. Since Woodrow Wilson, we can sincerely say that Hillary has all the traits that makes her a great Zionist leader.

Meanwhile, Senator Elizabeth Warren has taken an enormous task worthy of a person with good moral principles and a great leader. She is trying to reinstate the banking act of 1933 also known as the Glass-Steagall Act. She has reintroduced this legislation as the 21st Century Glass-Steagall Act of 2013. This legislation is to protect the people from Wall Street rapacious banking practices. The reason she is doing this is because the over promoted Dodd-Frank financial reform law. The Dodd-Frank law is favorable to the banks. But is largely ineffective to the consumer. That's why we need stronger legislation if we want to put a muzzle on these wolves. Let's point out that Representative Barney Frank a veteran in Congress. He served as chairperson in the House Financial Services Committee from (2007 to 2011). Representative Frank has served as chairperson but never did anything that could count as significant in his tenure. Representative Barney Frank failed to the taxpayers who pay his salary to restrict the wild overindulge of the Banking Cartel. Besides, Barney Frank is so confused that he is an atheist Jew. Anybody can tell you that's a contradiction of terms. That's what you call an oxymoron. But to add to his confusion, he married a man in 2012. I know I am being witty, but his professional traits didn't make him good Congressman Material. See what I mean by choosing poorly? Barney Frank dereliction of duty has made him a collaborator of the Zionist lobby. What can we say about Senator Chris Dodd, who served in Congress for thirty years. He served as chairperson of the Senate Committee on Banking, Housing and Urban Affairs from (2007 to 2011). He's an attorney and a lobbyist. For the record, to work as a lobbyist in Congress is a short definition of a full time Zionist shill. Again, Senator Dodd never did anything to slow down the bank's predatory lending practices. Chris Dodd has failed in his duties to the American people. But he has brilliantly succeeded as a lobbyist. After he left Congress he went on to become chairperson of the Motion Picture Association of America. But what does he know about motion pictures anyway? Is like asking how do you connect speed with bacon. But, that didn't matter. The MPAA is an organization under the complete influence and Zionist control. Start looking for The All Seeing Eye the next time you watch movies. With this much said: is there any reason we could expect them to give us an effective piece of legislation? On the other hand, Senator Warren pointed out the weaknesses in the Dodd-Frank law. She tells us the law fails to meet its goals. It does not include an effective oversight medium to ensure enforced regulations in the field. According to Warren, "the problem has actually gotten worse since the recession began. Bank consolidation is even more pronounced seven years after the crash." "Today, the four biggest banks are 30 percent larger than they were seven years ago. The five largest banks now hold more than half of the total banking assets in the country."

In other words, the Dodd-Frank Act works well for Wall Street that is. Just like the Federal Reserve continues to work well for Wall Street and terrible for the rest of us. The Glass-Steagall Act could significantly help us change the rules of the game in our favor. With the new Glass-Steagall Act. no bank would be too big to fail. It would lessen failures of the big banks breaking them down to small pieces protecting the deposits of the working class. Banks will not be too big to manage, too big to regulate, too big for trial, or too big for jail."

The Dodd-Frank Act. left the "too big" much untouched..." I wonder why!!

Let us go back to the Glass-Steagall Act of 1933. Let's remember that Carter Glass was the representative, Democrat of Virginia. He sponsored the Federal Reserve Act with Senator Robert Owen Democrat of Oklahoma. My guess is that Senator Carter Glass in 1933 must have felt some remorse after the stock market crash of 1929. Causing the big depression was a plunder for Wall Street and a shift of power for the Zionist. But it brought so much suffering, misery, famine in America. Carter Glass must have felt powerless to repeal the Federal Reserve. But at least he would try to protect the working class. He joined with Representative Henry Steagall. To help the consumers and subside the crisis, they brought this legislation to the floor. This legislation was to keep separated the traditional commercial banks. They are the ones which hold the checking and savings accounts of every working American. From the investment banks. These are the heavy rollers, those which make riskier bets. This was the response of Congress to the 1929 planned and calculated Stock Market crash.

For over fifty years. The Glass-Steagall Act of 1933 acted as the regulatory fire wall. This wedge between commercial and investing banks protected our economy from disasters like 2008. So, Who dared to remove the wall? Under the presidency of Bill Clinton. In 1999 the Gramm-Leach-Bliley Act took place to take apart the Glass-Steagall Act of 1933. Senator Phil Gramm is an economist, banker and I call him a sorcerer's apprentice. He earned to right to be among of the ten most wanted culprits of the collapse of 2008 by CNN Zionist Network. For his handy work and well-known tides with the banks, we can compare him to the late Zionist Senator Nelson Aldrich. The repeal of the Glass-Steagall Act in 1999. This event had its likenesses with the opposition creating the Federal Reserve in 1913. This time was Senator Byron Dorgan Democrat of N. Dakota. The only lonely voice that understood and warned the Senate if you go ahead with the Gramm-Leach-Bliley Act. Had the Glass-Steagall Act left intact. Americans wouldn't have suffered such enormous loss and hardship. The fleece to the consumers to satisfy Zionist Wall Street's insatiable greed wouldn't have happened.

With Larry Summer at the time the Secretary of the Treasury. The regulatory firewall of protection to our economy fell down just like the Berlin wall. We need to work to bring back the protecting wall that once served us well. At least to mitigate in part a future shock like the one in 2008. Break down the big banks in smaller parts makes sense. They will not be too big to fail and won't need taxpayer's money to bail them out. Is not exactly trying to repeal the Federal Reserve, but is a step we should work together to support. If we continue passing laws restricting more and more the movements of these Zionist crooks. Then, it's possible to regain our freedoms; it's possible to regain control of the government once again. As long as we have someone like Senator Elizabeth Warren the fight is not been lost, we are just beginning.

Senator Elizabeth Warren has been a Harvard law professor specializing in bankruptcy and personal finance. Back in 2004 she did an interview with Bill Moyers. In that interview she expressed her concerns for middle class families. She said "Families live in a very dangerous economic world than they did a generation ago, and we are heading for an economic disaster" She sure knew what she was talking about. Now from the Senate she gives us her story about how Washington works. She puts it this way:

"Washington doesn't do better because Washington isn't trying to do better" "the fundamental problem in our system is that

Washington works for those who can hire armies of lobbyist, armies of lawyers and get just the rules they want" "It doesn't work so well for American families". - Elizabeth Warren.

She mentioned armies of lobbyist. And who is the most important and powerful lobbyist group shedding money left and right? The Zionist Jewish lobbyist. It's no secret that Congress has an infestation of lobbyist going on for decades. Still, the Zionist Jewish lobbyist are the biggest with money and influence. So, why Senators Lindsey Graham and Ted Cruz had to slap around Chuck Hagel so much? All he said was the truth! The Zionist Jews do buy influence in Washington. It doesn't take a genius to figure this out if you pay attention. It should be obvious Voltaire's quote "tell me who you cannot criticize and I tell who is in control".

We need to go against scoundrels that helped to pass the Financial Modernization Act of 1999. People like Bill Clinton and Senator Phil Gramm. On that day president Clinton said.

"This is a day we can celebrate as an American day and that the Glass-Steagall law is no longer appropriate for the economy in which we live and today what we are doing is modernizing the financial service industry, tearing down these antiquated laws and granting banks significant new authority and this is a very good day for the United States".

Seriously Bill? You spoke like a true Zionist Deceitful Banker.

On this day Bill you dished out as much bull to the American people as Woodrow Wilson did when he signed the Federal Reserve into law. Like you Wilson believed he was providing a new World Order beginning with the United States. But in all fairness Clinton was only following what his Zionist masters wanted him to do. Clinton the Zionist stooge and poor excuse for President. Who doesn't know diddly squat about banking could only be regurgitating the line his masters told him to say. This Zionist tactic showed too height for Clinton's league anyway. What I mean is he jumped from governor of Arkansas to chief executive of the Federal Government. Do you think a mama and papa store manager qualifies to run a Wal-Mart Super center? This is what happens when we don't show concern in politics, we chose poorly, we chose Clinton we chose Busch, we chose Obama.

The 21st Century Glass-Steagall Act of 2013 is the answer to stop commercial and investment banking at the same time. These conflicts of interest have the tendency for banks to engage in excessive speculative activity. This is like making the little guys pay for the excessive loses of the heavy rollers. Not fair at all. Does this sound familiar? After Glass-Steagall Act was repealed in 1999. The bankers went on a binge thanks to Robert Rubin, Larry Summers, Senator Phil Gramm, and Bill Clinton. Good old Billy signed it into law just like Woodrow Wilson did with the Federal Reserve in 1913. History repeats itself, we have heard it a thousand times. But why we don't learn. It's because we live in apathy, of lack of concern, and indifference. We just pay no attention, and this is what the Zionists are counting on. We are like mushrooms to them. They keep us in the dark and feed us BS.

I hope when I finish writing this book there will more joining this just cause. More than a year has passed since Senator Warren introduced the Glass-Steagall Act. However, it is just collecting dust in the Senate Committee on Banking, Housing, and Urban Affairs. I don't know about you. But I am going to start writing to my Senator, or representative of my state. I will ask, better yet, demand He/She gets on board with this legislation because it's about justice and necessary. Without the return to the Glass-Steagall Act another great catastrophe like in 2008 is just a matter of time.

Chapter 5

What is the CFR?

(Council on Foreign Relations)

Before I decided to write about the CFR I went on a small survey to find out if people know about the CFR. Do you know that it is? Do you know what it does? Do you know what it stands for? Who created it and why. To my disappointment, no one gave me a good enough answer. Nobody passed the first question, much less the rest. So, I feel is necessary to write about this important organization. The CFR is the direct result of World War One. The history books records World War One passed as the war that should have ended all wars. At the end of WWI because The League of Nations did not take place the Zionist of London suffered a setback. Instead, they created The Royal Institute of International Affairs (RIIA) in 1919. From the book written by Gunther K. Russbache "The Art of Global Politics". We find that funding of the CFR came from J.P. Morgan, Bernard Baruch, Jacob Schiff, Paul Warburg, and John D. Rockefeller, among others. We already know this group. Most of these characters created the Federal Reserve at Jekyll Island. After that they moved to create the RIIA in London. Almost at the same time in Paris they worked creating the CFR for the United States. Just two years after creating the RIIA the CFR took place for the first time in New York City on July 1921. The CFR received founding from the same group of Zionist that organized the RIIA. Among them was the ex-secretary of the State Elihu Root. He was a powerful corporate lawyer who served under President Theodore Roosevelt. Root served as Secretary of War, and was a U.S. Senator. It was his privilege to head the first Council on Foreign Relations. Added note. He was a fake Jew and a Zionist collaborator.

The CFR like the RIIA both powerful organizations appear instead of the failed Liege of Nations. In London and in Paris the Zionist elite saw the need to have the CFR in America in two cities. Washington, D.C. and New York. Under the disguise of a nonprofit organization the CFR is a think tank capable to gather the most prominent wealthy and powerful people. Among them, you will find bankers, lawyers, professors, and senior media figures. Through the CFR ranks have passed senior politicians, more than a dozen Secretaries of State, and CIA directors. It started out with no more than 150 members, today it is a 4900-member organization. The CFR specializes in U.S. foreign policy and international affairs. Better yet, they dictate the US foreign policy. Hillary Clinton while Secretary of State said it.

"It's good to have the CFR down the street from the Department of State. She added, we get a lot of advice from the Council, so this means I don't have this far to go; to be told what we should be doing".

This is Hillary Clinton, secretary of State speaking at the CFR in Washington DC. She is openly admitting she gets advice from the CFR. But what makes your jaw drop is the CFR tells Hillary what to do! This of course makes you wonder. Who's is running the show? Who pulls the strings of the US foreign policy? Let's put this into perspective. The CFR is like a private club of influential people. But they have no governmental authority at all. Yet, you have the Secretary of State admit they tell her what to do? The reason Hillary can say this heart stopping; breath taken truths is because she knows we are oblivious. The average citizen who does not know any better may think Hillary is taking about another government agency. Therefore, it is okay. No, it's not okay at all!... You see, this is why we need to do these things and connect the dots. So, next time we hear something like this coming out of her mouth we can challenge her. We can ask her: Who do you work for Hillary? If you said the CFR tells you what to do. Is our next President taking orders from the CFR too? I mean, If the CFR is Zionist country and Hillary gets her orders from them. What can we say about Congress, the White House, the Supreme Court.

Let's stick with the State Department just a little longer. Here is the ex-wife of a USMC Colonel Kay Griggs. She tells us of the degree of infiltration the Zionists have archived in the State Department Middle East Region.

"I went to the State Department near East section and found. There was not one single Palestinian. Not one single Moslem religious, Saudi, Jordanian, not one Christian Protestant. Not one Roman Catholic, not one plain old American. Every single person from all those offices were either Zionist, Israeli, whatever. They had pictures all over the wall Israel, Israel, Israel. They had magazines Israel Today. I was given a copy of one. There were yarmulkes (meaning skullcap in Yiddish) and Israeli writing. In other words. I asked one of the women after having gone through 4 or 5 of these offices. I said as I wanted to know where the Palestinian office was. She said: "Oh. We handle all that." "Oh. We handle all that."

Hearing all that was enough to convince Kay Griggs the total domination the Israeli Zionists have in the State Department. How can we possibly issue a fair policy in the Middle East if we have Israeli Zionist domination in our State Department? It's time we start to examine, clean house, find out who is who and run them through the Zionist strainer. Only then, we can begin to take our country back and make better choices for America. For Hillary the Zionist is irrelevant to consult the Foreign Affairs Committee unless of course they are also a Zionist.

The CFR goals is to extend its influence in the United States and abroad. Through various methods of persuasion the CFR promotes globalization. Also, free trade, reducing financial regulations on transnational corporations. This is in contrast with what the Nobel Economics Prize winner Mohammad Yanus said about globalization. In his words he said:

"I support globalization and believe, it can bring more benefits to the poor than its alternative. But it must be the right kind of globalization. To me, globalization is like a hundred-lane highway crisscrossing the world. If it is a free-for-all highway, its lanes will be taken over by the giant trucks from powerful economies. Bangladeshi rickshaw will be thrown off the highway. In order to have a win-win globalization, we must have traffic rules, traffic police, and traffic authority for this global highway. The rule of "strongest takes it all" must be replaced by rules that ensure that

the poorest have a place and piece of the action, without being elbowed out by the strong. Globalization must not become financial imperialism."

Yet, the Council on Foreign Relations is the flagship of Geopolitical and Financial Imperialism. Because the members of the CFR are under the Zionist agenda of world domination, their efforts have brought us NAFTA and the European Union. The Council on Foreign Relations has put strenuous effort to develop policy recommendations that reflect these goals. It's the summit where all the super rich and the VIPs meet to develop and dictate policies. If you were a hunter you'll think you're on safari. The lion, the tiger, the elephant, the donkey. Oh My.!! You'll be among government officials, global business leaders and prominent members of Congress. The industrialist, the intelligence, and foreign-policy makers, they all gather there to discuss international affairs. The CFR represents the power center where the big decisions are made. Forget Congress, forget, the Oval Office. Forget the Supreme Court. The CFR comprise members of the most important corporations and branches of government. David Rockefeller is among the founders, his think tank "David Rockefeller Studies Program." publishes the bimonthly journal Foreign Affairs. This is David Rockefeller the Internationalist. The one who says I stand guilty of conspiring against the United States

Should this conspirator have the power to influence presidential decisions by recommending foreign policy? The White House, the diplomatic community, and The State Department. If David needs someone testifying before Congress, he has minions to do his bidding. The same applies when David interferes the mainstream media for his own personal gain. Remember he who controls the printed page controls the thinking of the age. David shapes public opinion with his publication Foreign Affairs.

The one way to describe the CFR, that it is a colossal Power Center. Would you believe the CFR is a non-profit organization? I say sure! In a pig's eye. Still, for a non-profit organization they run their affairs so secretive. According to it's website, any documents the CFR produces remain sealed for twenty five years before they publish. It's verifiable, you can read on their website. There is nothing innocent or transparent to a non-profit organization like the CFR. It's linked with the most powerful secret societies in the world, But that does not matter because the Zionist control them all. At the CFR; the members of the inner circle are Zionist and the rest Zionist collaborators. I mean, you can call me irresponsible. But for all practical purposes. This is your Zionist Headquarters of the Shadow government of the United States. Once you become a member of the CFR your political affiliation does not matter. Whether you are a Democrat or a Republican you can throw that out the window, it is just irrelevant. Under the duress of a few dominant men like Woodrow Wilson mentioned, Democrats, Republicans work together for the CFR not for the People of The United States. Once you are a member the CFR will tell you what to do, just like Hillary Clinton said.

The CFR can gather the cream of the crop members of our government, industries, military, and intelligence. You don't think they are going to meet just to chit-chat and drink tea? Do you? The CFR with the RIIA in London work in tandem. They are solid evidence of what Carroll Quigley wrote in his book the Anglo-American Establishment. By the same talking, the Federal Reserve and the Bank of England also work in tandem. Do you remember chairman Bernanke went to London for a trip of negotiations? Perhaps it was more like reporting to his bosses. It should strike strange the United States regardless of being the world's only super power. Still, has to check in like a colony to its old master.

The following is a short list of members of the Council on Foreign Relations. I've chosen some of the most easy to recognize names. It shows how far the Zionist connection goes and who works for America and who works for a foreign power.

I will start with the list of CIA Directors.

Water Smith, William Coley, Richard Helms, Allen Dulles, James Schlesinger, George Busch Sr., Stansfield Turner, William Casey, William Webster, Robert Gates, George Tenet, Michael Hayden

Secretary of Defense

James Forrestal, George Marshall, Charles Wilson, Robert McNamara Melvin Laird, Eliot Richardson, James Lesinger, Harold Brown, Caspar Weinburger, Richard Chaney, William Perry, William Cohen, Donald Rumsfeld

Secretary of State

Dean Rusk, Robert Lansing, Frank Kellogg, Henry Stimson, Cordell Hull, George Marshall, Dean Atkinson, John Foster Dulles, William Rogers, Henry Kissinger, Cyrus Vance, Edmund Muskie, Alexander Haig, George Schulz, James Baker, Lawrence. Eagleburger, Warren Christopher, Madeleine Albright, Collin Powell, Condoleezza Rice, Hillary Clinton, John Kerry.

I would venture to say all the biggest corporations in America are members of the CFR. The list is too long, but if you know household names you can make your own list.

Last but not least Presidents of the Unites States.

Herbert Hoover, Dwight Eisenhower, Richard Nixon, Gerard Ford James Carter, George H. Busch, George W. Busch, William Clinton.

Rumor has it that Barack Obama is a member of the CFR, he gets support from them. However, we know that his wife Michelle Obama is a member of the CFR. Go figure.

I think this is an impressive list of important people who have served in public office. But they have served under the protecting/controlling umbrella of the CFR. Still, out of these bunch I want to bring about the Dulles duo. Better knows as the John Foster Dulles, Secretary of State and Allen Dulles, Central Intelligence Agency director. These two brothers became brilliant attorneys. Allen graduated out of George Washington University Law School in 1926. Allen and Foster Dulles were part of the founders team the created the CFR. Allen was present in Paris with the founders team to discuss the forming the CFR. He became CFR director in 1927. Allen went to work with his brother Foster at the prestigious law firm Sullivan and Cromwell in New York. There the two brothers stayed at Sullivan and Cromwell for decades to become rich and powerful. The Dulles brothers give us another opportunity to connect the dots. We can prove the Zionist financed the Nazis through the CFR and with the Dulles brother's aid. We said it before. You don't need to be Jewish to be a Zionist. Companies like GM, Ford, Standard Oil, IBM under the Zionist spell Supported Nazi Germany war machine. Out of this group only Ford supported Hitler's policy against the Jews. He made no distinction between Jews and Zionist, but we do.

Now that we know the CFR is your regular Zionist country and the Dulles brothers were members at the beginning. How could the CFR over-looked dealing John Foster Dulles made with Hitler's Germany? Assuming the Zionist were Jews first and Zionist later they would not have allowed it. Shockingly, the Zionist force you to act a Zionist first, and a Jew later. But the Zionist had two excellent agents in the Dulles brothers who did their bidding in spades. They protected Zionist interest in the United States and in Nazi Germany at the same time. It didn't matter the millions of Jews, they were going to put at risk. To cause suffering and death is of no importance to them as long they profit and advance their world domination agenda. They went ahead and caused to kill millions of their own people during World War Two. Part of the herd I guess. But somebody had to pay. Somebody has to take the blame. So, they made Adolf Hitler their scapegoat. The rest is Zionist history, of course. Experts in outlandish stories suggest these people may not be human. For sure, they don't act like humans. They have shown a degree of depravity and cruelty beyond understanding. For most of the 1920 and '30s, Allen Dulles worked with his brother Foster at the Wall Street law firm of Sullivan & Cromwell. There they learned to cut deals for the most important and wealthy corporations in America. Corporations run by Zionist Jews who needed to expand their influence abroad. This long and successful practice contributed the Dulles brothers to assimilate an inaccurate believe. They were convinced that by defending the interest of the corporations they were defending the interest of America.

Unfortunately, this idea still prevails in the minds the public. For example, the biggest oil companies are present in the Middle East to control the oil supply. Whenever there a crisis the President tells us we need to be there to defend our American interest. Forgive me, but since when are the big oil companies under government control? When the government sends troops to the Middle East is to defend the corporate interest and the oil companies. The Zionist use our troops like cannon fodder to achieve their goals. It's the blood of our soldiers that helps the Zionist like Rockefeller (Exxon owner) to rake more profits and we don't get even get a break at the pump. The next time you see the sign NO BLOOD FOR OIL! You'll know what they are talking about.

It was in 1951 that they suffered their first defeat in Iran. The elected Prime Minister of Iran, Mohammad Mossadegh decided to nationalize the oil fields. The presence of more English than American oil companies were possible by the efforts of Sullivan & Cromwell. This didn't look good in the eyes of the Dulles brother's clients. Although they were corporate lawyers their behavior was more like an economic hit man.

In 1950 in Guatemala a free election took place. The president, elected Jacobo Arbenz Guzman represented the will of the people for the first time. His land reform efforts resulted in intervening the United Fruit Company, another client of the Dulles brothers and another defeat. The Dulles brothers held a grudge in Iran and in Guatemala. With their reputation as economic hit men they itched for a change to fix these aberrations. So, with the CFR and the Zionist influence in Washington the Dulles brothers went to work on payback. In 1953 John Foster Dulles became Secretary of State and Allen Dulles became CIA Director. The first time in American history that two brothers were in charge of the overt operations under the Secretary of State and the covert operations under the CIA. Little did the world know that this unique, powerful combination. Little the world thought of these shrewd brothers and the CFR would help to shape in large the second half of the twentieth century. As soon as President Eisenhower took office Allen Dulles went work in designing a plan to overthrow the Prime Minister of Iran. With the approval of Eisenhower and the English government Dulles began fulfilling the plan starting on July 1953. By December 1953 Mohammad Mossadegh would be no longer in power and received 3 years in jail. The Western friendly Mohammad Reza Pahlavi, returned to take over as the Shah of Iran until 1979. On that year the Shah sought refuge in the US and the Islamic Revolution of the Ayatollah Khomeini took hold. Thanks to the Dulles brothers unconstitutional and illegal coup d'etat in Iran our relations with Iran are lukewarm at best. The Iranians do not trust us. Can you blame them? The CIA Director under orders from President Eisenhower both CFR members under Zionist control. In conspiracy with the English decided to overthrow the legitimate government of Iran. This shameful act is for the sole purpose of protecting the unfair exploitation of Iranian oil. Do you still wonder why they would offer resistance? Today the world Zionist press paints a picture that Iran is seeking nuclear weapons to destroy Israel. No, I think it's the other way around. Iran knows behind the Jews are the Zionist and they remember what they have done in their country. They know that Israel is a Zionist State. Iran is desperate in trying to develop the only bargaining chip that can keep Israel and the US from bombing Tehran.

What the Dulles brother did in Guatemala was something similar. It was the first covert operation of the young CIA in Central America for the purpose to overthrow the legitimate government of President Arbenz. Their excuse was that they assumed he acted under orders from the Kremlin. After President Jacobo Arbenz Guzman was deposed 1954. President Eisenhower thought that this would send a clear message to the Soviets. There will be no communism expansion in Central America as long as I am President.

Great. Thank you Mr. president.

But what about the Guatemalans? Why couldn't the Dulles brothers recognize that they were fighting for their freedom? Isn't that what we in America stand for? You see. That was another day of shame in the annals of our history. On that day, they didn't act the American way, they acted the Zionist way.

As a result, the friendly Carlos Castillo Armas assumed control of the government thanks to the Dulles and the CIA under the CFR. The Dulles brothers reestablished promoting American interests in Guatemala. Better yet, they reinstated their client's control in Guatemala. Clearly the purpose of this operation had nothing to do with defending American interest. Instead, they defended the rights of the, exploiters, the slave drivers, the expansionist. Those we cannot criticize, I sure you know the type. The government of president Jacobo Arbenz Guzman couldn't be a threat to America, even if he had tried. In fact, Arbenz was an allied a leader who fights for freedom and democracy. Had the Zionist influence not been so pervasive in the minds of the Dulles brothers they would have left President Arbenz alone. However, the result of the Dulles grouch sacrificed the Guatemalan people with thirty-five year civil war, more than 200,000 deaths.

Nice work Allen!

But it didn't stop here. John Foster Dulles arrives in 1954 in Geneva, Switzerland for a world leaders convention. They gather there because France had reached its limit and had to face losing Vietnam to Ho Chi Minh. They realized that Ho Chi Minh has been just too powerful and popular that he was impossible to defeat. Winston Churchill was there and he agreed with the French. But that wasn't good enough for John Dulles. When he realized that he was alone in his belief he did something impossible to believe for an American diplomat. He walked out of the summit. Immediately, he returned to the United States and started to work with his brother Allen on a plan to defeat Ho Chi Minh. Tragically nobody swayed John Dulles misguided resolve to overthrow Ho Chi Minh. Because had John Foster Dulles not been so obtuse, so narrow-minded, so fanatic, we could have steered clear of the Vietnam conflict. We could have saved 55,000 American lives and more than 2,000,000 Vietnamese could have been alive. This is another piece of history omitted to teach in schools and we need to know.

Thank you John. This time you outdid yourself.

The Vietnam war showed us how far apart we acted from the American way. We acted in the Zionist way in Vietnam and it has only brought us shame and sorrow. Because the Zionist thrives on conflict the Vietnam war provided another rich source to make much money. In fact, There is much evidence that points to David Rockefeller doing weapons deals with the former Soviet Union. He invested in factories that build combat vehicles, weapons, and ammunition. David Rockefeller knew perfectly well the Soviets would supply these vehicles and weapons to North Vietnam to kill American soldiers. This is what you can expect from an unscrupulous vermin like David Rockefeller and his cronies.

You may think the Dulles brothers were some Godless individuals, deprived of any teaching of the Christian faith. Only men Godless men or fanatics could have acted in such a despicable way and commit such a wicked crime against humanity. Well... No, nothing could be further from the truth. The Dulles brothers came out of Presbyterian Calvinism. They grew up in a parsonage; their father was a clergyman they had to go to services every day, three times on Sundays. They took notes to discuss the sermons with their father. They sang hymns at home and spent much time in prayer. These two were your regular choirboys. However, I believe this excessive Christian indoctrination made the Dulles brothers believe that God is white. They turned out narrow-minded and shortsighted about the world. They saw the world in two ways: The good Christians and the heathens and savages. They adopted the Roman way of thinking, everybody outside of Roman law was a savage or barbarian. The Dulles brothers under this doctrine, felt they couldn't be sitting at home hoping for the triumph of good. No, this wasn't good enough to them, they had to go out into the world and make sure that good triumphed. But for the love of God. The good they did caused more misfortune, more despair and death than the two atomic bombs dropped on Hiroshima and Nagasaki. Sure, they believe that they acted correctly in the name of Christianity, but this is also what you call acting as religious fanatics. Still, we act so surprised and so hurt by the desperate actions of the suppressed people of the world trying to defend their own political or religious convictions. We call these people terrorists. Now, this does not mean that I wish to clear those radical groups that are seeking to kill Americans and its allies. But what I wish to point out is the actions of people like the Dulles brothers have helped to create these groups out of resentment for our terrible foreign policy. In all truthfulness, the United States does not control its foreign policy. If you recall Hillary Clinton, while she was Secretary of State, she admits, its the CFR that tells her what to do. Tragically we have to admit, the US foreign policy for decades reflects a Zionist policy to create conflict and profit.

I am sure you find obvious the reasons for opposing the CFR. This Zionist power center has links to many other powerful groups. Organizations like the Trilateral Commission, the Bilderburg Group, and many others. I am not too interested in those groups that work outside our borders, but those we have running here on US soil. First things first. We must put our own house in order. We must erase the Zionist infestation from our government. Then, after we clean house we might help those who seek our help. **Like President Jackson said to the bankers I say to the Zionist and the Zionist shills. "I intend to rout you out and by the eternal God, I will rout you out."**

The last Great President of the United States John F. Kennedy had this to say about organizations like the CFR that like to operate in secret within our society. On April 27, 1961 at the Waldoff Astoria hotel in New York City, the American Newspaper Publishers Association invited President Kennedy to speak. This meeting took place only ten days after the failed rebellion of Allen Dulles at the Bay of Pigs. On this occasion, President Kennedy delivered one of the most powerful speeches to warn us about the clear and present dangers of the secret monolithic government ruling the world. He called them repugnant, that they do not have a place to exist in a free society. In only nineteen minutes President Kennedy explained the world he lived-in and the treats he faced, and he asked the press to do what is required of them. A free, concise, impartial journalism. I urge you to hear his speech in its entirety on the Internet archives.

Reflections

The economist Paul Samuelson firmly believed in the awesome power money and the economy is to be at the bank's control. Thus, in his view he would find no conflict surrendering the power of money at the hands of the Bankers. Milton Freeman another brilliant economist had an opposite view. He said. "Money matters are too important to be left at the hands of the bankers". I completely agree with Milton Freeman. Time over time the bankers have failed to keep the economy stable. In the course, they have become richer and richer, further increasing the gap between rich and poor. After one hundred years of tyrannical ruling, it is now imperative to seek to lessen this gruesome disparity, if we want a better world, with more justice, and prosperity. As citizens of this great country we must unite to introduce a new financial scheme we can depend on. If we wish to live with Liberty and Peace as out banner we must guarantee us economic stability that would bring a peaceful future for our children. I suggest we start treating the power of money with the same zealous we treat nuclear power and nuclear weapons.

Money is a tool man has known for many centuries. Still, money is also a power source no one can control. If we want to keep it from doing harm to us we need to confront human greed and put shackles on it. If we can condemn vengeance, surely we can condemn greed. A crime committed out of vengeance is punishable by law. Crimes committed by bankers for greed must be punishable by law too. We have known fire for a thousand years. We know it can keep us warm at home but can also burn the house when out of control. We can assume the likenesses when we talk about money. It can provide for us the economic stability we want. Given to the wrong hands it can devastate millions of homes like a tsunami. Since Amschel Rothschild declared.

"give me control of the nation's money and I care not who makes the laws"

This arrogant and immoral quote from a Rothschild Zionist was a warning. Sadly, never made It in the minds of our functionaries. In fact, our founding fathers failed to prescribe a much stronger legislation for the power of money. Although Thomas Jefferson, and James Madison worn us, unfortunately they fell in deaf ears. As time has passed, the stakes have grown higher. The financial crisis of the nineteenth century and the twentieth century will be small game compare to what is coming. If we do not start tiding the screws on these Zionist vandals, they will continue tiding the noose on us even further. The bankers always like to play a game of strategy. But is more like cat and mouse, where they are the cat and we are the mouse. Their way to do business is to enjoy the authority, without the responsibility. Their wicked genius made possible the banking fraud we have today, and because it is flawed, it cannot continue forever. We cannot afford to have a banking industry where the masters feel they can perform with impunity. Is wrong to see bankers robbing the public and the taxpayer come to their rescue. No sir. That is tyranny. It cannot find justification in the American way of doing justice. As long as this scheme of tyranny prevails, we are the slaves. Isn't that what we call to the citizens of North Korea, or Cuba? China is the great experiment of what awaits us in the New World Order.

It is necessary to start changing our ideas about money as a source of ruthless power. Up to now the bad thing accomplished with the money power outweighs the good things accomplished with money by one hundred to one. Starting with the basic idea, we need money to survive to the realization that money carries the intrinsic power to build or destroy. Unless we grow and change our frame of thought about money, and after that we take it away from those who seek our slavery and destruction. For sure we are heading for much bigger global financial catastrophes like a devastating nuclear attack. This our future as long as this awesome power continues in the wrong hands. They have the arsenal ready. Those wizards of Wall Street and London, have produced Derivatives. They are obscure financial contracts designed to produce financial devastation like an atomic bomb. They have labeled them (WMD) Weapons of Mass Deception. These are the latest instruments in the destructive financial arsenal of Wall Street and London. We should take warning from two of America's most famous investor Warren Buffett, and Bill Gross, the manager of PIMCO. A multibillion-dollar bond fund. These two investors protested against derivatives, calling them "financial weapons of mass destruction." They claim that derivatives enable corporate treasurers to gamble with shareholders money. These derivatives are what we must begin to dismantle like toxic waste. The old financial scheme must be destroy just like obsolete warheads to make way to a new era of financial responsibility. The future financial tycoons must learn from the start the most important lesson. Every financial tycoon should live by these words. "If you have the authority you have to have responsibility." We must do away with printing money out of nothing. That means adios Federal Reserve. That is so crooked an irresponsible that slowly it's bringing the country to ruin. We must do away with fractional deposits. How can we allow people to lend money that they don't have and collect interest on it. As a result, they collect more money than those who actually do the work. But wait a minute. The money that they print actually has support and you know what that is? Our backs. Yes yours and mine and every body else. You see. We are their slaves from the moment we're born. We are a commodity to them. Okay fine. But with this rationality you would think that they would want to take better care of us. I mean make medical care more affordable. But the reality is medical insurance is further out of our reach. Pharmaceutical drugs kill just as many people as the illegal drugs. The food we eat has chemicals harmful to our health. The vaccines we used to trust are now in question. It is like if they want to cut out a whole bunch of us. Don't they? Well, it looks like an apocalyptic plan. The NOW would like to Reducing the world population to around 600 million or less. We can find evidence of this evil plan at the Mysterious Guidestones in Elbert County Georgia. These monoliths are also known as the American Stonehenge. Our struggle cannot stop it we must continue until we cut the head of the snake. We must start with the Zionist collaborators, then the families in control of the money supply. We can find if the number of deaths all over the world by natural disasters is greater or equal to the number of deaths caused by war. Or if the number of deaths caused by war are greater than or equal to the number of death by natural disasters. All the more reason to regulate the power of money. We must regulate the power of money with the same rigor and vigilance we regulate a nuclear plant. With the same restrictive measures we manage our nuclear weapons. We know these Zionist bankers have been handling this power with recklessness and impunity. Well then, it's time that we the people must act and take it away from them. We can begin by supporting Elizabeth Warren. Her project the 21st Century Glass-Steagall Act of 2013 as I said before is not going to repeal the Federal Reserve by is a small step in the right direction. The idea is to change our preconceived ideas about money. No one or no small group of people have the right to monopolize this power for their own benefit. We have seen it in the hands of the Zionist. These gangsters have used the power of money only to bring instability, confusion, misery. Just after the Federal Reserve we have seen disasters, famine, and unnecessary wars throughout the world. It's time to learn their game and outfox the foxes. Is not going to be easy. But nothing worth having is. The Zionist will plot and wage war against us. They know to achieve their goals they must keep control of the supreme power, the power of money. When we are successful and we will. The financial monstrosity they have created for the last one hundred year will end. The moment more and more people become aware and start protesting. Why not you; write to your members of Congress or

Senator. Start telling your Politicians in Congress to reject legislation that favors the Zionist Jewish lobbyist. When the Will of the American People starts firing those Zionist collaborators they will know we mean business. Start asking whether a candidate is a Zionist or not. If the Zionist feel bold enough to ask whether our Secretary of Defense will defend Israel we sure have the right to ask; why should we? And you know what? Zionist supremacy can go to hell.

If you have any doubt about the Zionist influence at the highest levels of Wall Street and Washington. Just remember Eliot Spritzer. He became attorney general of the state of New York in 1999 and then governor of the State of New York by a landslide. People who liked him thought that he could have been the first Jewish president of the United States. Eliot became the Sheriff of Wall Street and took on to change the way Wall Street works. He went after environmental abuses, went after the insurance company fraud. His misdeed was to go after sex with a young woman in a hotel in Washington DC and that was his downfall. I say to you those who are free of sin, go ahead and throw the first stone. On the other hand, Bill Clinton who gave the Zionist the Gramm-Leach-Bliley Act. had sex in the White House Oval Office he showed complete disrespect for the presidency. Lied about it to his wife and the entire world. To this day he walks all praised and dignified. He still travels the country giving speeches and charges outrageous amounts of money. Nevertheless, who are his crowd? Bill Clinton can only gather a bunch of gullible, simpleminded, people who want to hear him speak worthless rhetoric. That's Billy. What is wrong with this picture? Still, this is how Zionist rewards their friends. Moreover, how they punish those who dare to act against them like Eliot Spitzer and Elizabeth Warren.

Do not let the Zionist propaganda influence you no more; challenge it, and do your own research. You will find out In the words of the Israeli ex-minister of Education Shulamit Aloni (1992-1993). She was interviewed on radio by Amy Goodman and when she asked. "Often, when there is dissent expressed in the United States against policies of the Israeli government, people here are called "anti-Semitic" What is your response to that as an Israeli Jew?"

Shulamit Answered:

"Well it's a trick, we always use it. When from Europe someone is criticizing Israel we bring up the Holocaust. when in this country someone is criticizing Israel then they are anti-Semitic. And the organization (she means AIPAC) is strong and has a lot of money. The ties between America and the American Jewish establishment are very strong. They have power, which is okay. They are talented people, and the attitude is "Israel my country Right or Wrong" and they are not ready to hear criticism. I mean it's very easy to blame people who criticize certain acts of the Israeli government as anti-Semitic to bring up the Holocaust and the suffering of the Jewish people that justifies everything we do to the Palestinians."

Now I have no more words, except I rest my case. I think the next time someone calls me anti-Semitic. First, I want ask. Can you prove you have Semitic blood running through your veins? I stand 9 out of 10 chances he/she is not. The true Jews look more than Africans from Ethiopia and not blonde and blue eyes; those are Khazarians. These are white Europeans from the Caucasian Mountains than anything else. These people adopted the Jewish religion by political decision and not a heart-felt conviction. Later they invaded Europe and became what we know as the European Jew. Today the few true Jews who live in Israel speak and march against the Zionist Jews. Therefore, chances are that if someone is accusing you of anti-Semitic is not a Jew. More likely is a despicable Zionist hell-bent into bringing you to utter submission. If you think that Adolph Hitler was bad, these people make the Nazis look like quire boys.

In the bigger scheme of things it is the eternal battle between good and evil. Didn't we learn in Sunday school the devil is the master of deception? That God allowed the Devil to rule the world? Sure thing, and even more important these Zionist have believed these stories well enough and long enough to make them a reality. Proof of is the return of the nation of Israel once again. Forth told by the bible but brought to reality by the Zionist Rothschild family. We have believed the power of God brought back Israel. The truth is Israel is the product of the despicable Zionist influence. The condition God gave to Israel was to be obedient. However, we know in Israel by their actions they are far from it.

Hopefully you find this book serves you as a revelation and can entice you to continue your learning. Now that you have read it you should be more effective in identifying who are the enemies of the United States and battle them smart and successful. Serving in the United States Navy I took the oath. "That I would defend the United States of America from enemies foreign and domestic". I have served with honor and I have been honorable discharged. To this day do not remember that oath has ever been discharged. Therefore, it is my duty and the duty of every citizen to do his/her part. The Zionist vermin will be defeated and eliminated. Only then the United States will take its rightful place as a beacon of liberty and democracy. It will be a republic again in a more just and peaceful world.